Crashing the Commission

Crashing the Commission

Confessions of a University Twit

a memoir

Mark D. Harmon

Tellico Books
Oak Ridge, Tennessee

Copyright © 2011 by Mark D. Harmon

All rights reserved. No portion of this book may be reproduced in any form or by any means, including electronic storage and retrieval systems, without explicit, prior written permission of the publisher, except for brief passages excerpted for review and critical purposes.

Cover Photograph Copyright © 2007 by Jon Gustin

Tellico Books
an imprint of the Iris Publishing Group, Inc

www.tellicobooks.com

Design: Robert B Cumming, Jr.

Library of Congress Cataloging-in-Publication Data

Harmon, Mark D. (Mark Desmond), 1957-
 Crashing the commission : confessions of a university twit : a memoir / Mark D. Harmon.
   p. cm.
 Includes bibliographical references.
 ISBN 978-1-60454-003-1 (pbk. : alk. paper)
  1. Harmon, Mark D. (Mark Desmond), 1957- 2. Politicians—Tennessee—Knox County—Biography. 3. County officials and employees—Tennessee—Knox County—Biography. 4. Knox County (Tenn.)—Officials and employees—Biography. 5. Knox County (Tenn.). County Commission—Biography. 6. Knox County (Tenn.)—Politics and government—21st century. 7. Knox County (Tenn.)—Social conditions—21st century. 8. College teachers—Tennessee—Knoxville—Biography. 9. University of Tennessee, Knoxville—Faculty—Biography. I. Title.
 F443.K6H37 2011
 324.2092—dc23

2011033820

This book is dedicated to two remarkable men and nine phenomenal women, starting with Jolie Bonavita, Drucilla Stills and Dru's predecessor Star Matthews. These unheralded commission secretaries worked diligently in public service and made us look better than we were.

My wife Becky was infinitely patient with me as we went through this unusual world together. My grandmothers, Claire Rose Hawthorne Holzer and Lillian Sarah Desmond Harmon, were important early inspirations to me. My mother, Claire Harmon, as well as my sister, Pam Glasgow, and her daughter Kelley inspire me to this day. My late father Jerome Harmon taught me the patience and humor that proved to be necessary for this adventure, and my nephew Mack Glasgow joins me in awe of our family of strong women.

I'm grateful to Becky, Larry Van Guilder, Brian Griffin, and Dr. Barbara Moore, all of whom read early drafts and made helpful suggestions. I'm also grateful to Jon Gustin for providing several photos used in this book. Laura Cole and Carla Wyrick were kind in providing additional photos. Robert B. Cumming and Beto Cumming at Tellico Books saw value in this project and helped make it happen. Also, throughout my time on county commission I've been a "big" in the Big Brothers program to Levi Lacey. He was a great kid and is growing into a thoughtful young man.

Contents

Prologue: *Looking into a Hole* 9

1: *Birth of a Political and University Twit* 13

2: *Roaring at the Lions Club* 21

3: *Two-a-Day Drills, Two-fers, and Too Much* 25

4: *God, Gays, Guns, and Goofy Government* 34

5: *Molly Ivins and Black Wednesday* 41

6: *Trial and Tribulation* 60

7: *It Just Buffoons Me* 68

8: *Spiritual Home* 73

9: *Hate and the Church Shooting / Standing on the Side of Love* 83

10: *Land Whoa!* 91

11: *BZA — Cooler Than It Sounds* 97

12: *Baby you can drive my county take-home car* 106

13: *No Comment* 112

14: *The Moments When It Is Worth All the Trouble* 115

15: *Roundin' Third and Headin' Home* 118

16: *NIMBY, the Homeless, and Political Identity* 121

17: *Decommissioned* 126

Notes 134

Prologue:
Looking into a Hole

The power of the past is nowhere more apparent than in the field of rural and local government. Those whose lives are rooted to the soil of a native town, township, or village have become immunized through the centuries to the advances of political science.

—Arthur W. Bromage,
"Notes on Rural Local Government," 1931.[1]

It's deep into an August evening. The sky is pink and purple in the extended sunset, and Knoxville City Councilman Bob Becker is showing me a hole. It's at least six-feet deep, and was dug by the homeowner in search of a drainage pipe that crosses his property. The pipe isn't working. The back yard floods in even modest rainfalls. In serious downpours a puddle of water creeps within inches of the homeowner's house.

I struggle to say something more intelligent than, "Yep, that's a hole." I needn't bother. Bob, the homeowner, and a neighbor are in an animated and detailed conversation. They rattle off details about how the repaving of a nearby church parking lot had redirected even more water in their direction. They speak about various city and water company officials by first name. At one point, Bob confides "Sad to say it, but you may have to sue us at the city to get the attention you need."

This likely was Bob's way of introducing me to the oddities of local governance. I had been elected only about ten days earlier. That election had come as a surprise to many, including Bob. Early on Election Day he had confided to my opponent, "I don't think Mark can beat you." I joked with

Bob about the useful misdirection. The backyard water discussion he arranged nicely foreshadowed the succeeding years on Knox County Commission. We repeatedly would struggle with storm water, clash over land use, and muddle though a succession of lawsuits.

"I can't believe anyone votes for these guys," says an attendee later at a community forum, referencing my colleagues on commission. "Oh, no," I correct, "if there's one thing these guys have in common, it's they can get people, at least in their district, to like them." Indeed, that may be the only thing these guys have in common. I started my time on commission serving with two used car salesmen, an insurance agent, a teacher, retirees, etc. It was not a good cross-section of the community but it was not monolithic.

The dynamics of interaction among this group can change quickly. Take the case of John Mills, thought by some to be acerbic, even mean. He ran the Intergovernmental Committee meetings for speed, barely withholding his exasperation with questions I raised in my first few months on commission. However, I sent him a Christmas card. He thrice thanked me, and ever since has been as kind and courteous as possible.

If there is another defining characteristic of the Knox County Commissioners, it is they rarely, if ever, turn off the schmooze. Even when greeting or interacting with one another, an extraordinary degree of backslapping and complimenting goes on. While it may vary in sincerity, it is necessary. Grudges can be counterproductive. The commissioner you greatly offend on one vote, you may need minutes later on the next vote.

On a national level there are hundreds of thousands of us, otherwise normal people who for some reason throw ourselves into the nasty, confusing world of local politics. Some of us have been lucky enough to prevail in low-turnout elections that usually slip beneath the radar of local television, radio, and newspapers.

That's when things get even more bizarre. We find ourselves serving on school boards, city councils, and county commissions, trying to make sense and to make good choices on school-attendance policies or zoning changes or the pay of police officers and firefighters.

These are important matters, but a strange inverse rule begins to take hold: the smaller the matter, the larger the invective of the argument. People pleasantly may "agree to disagree" on wedge-driving national issues like abortion or military spending, but get near apoplectic with each other over whether concrete or plastic is best for storm water pipes, or whether traffic circles or speed humps are best for slowing drivers on neighborhood streets, or whether a neighborhood should be rezoned into a different high school.

Things like political party and ideological philosophy are poor predictors of what will happen, but historical animosities and friendships as well as local power blocs have much more predictive power. While our county commissioners have fixed interests and habits, the group dynamics change slightly with every meeting and every issue. Any hope of success requires a skill at "reading the room" or "counting to ten," a shorthand for vote success; ten out of nineteen is a majority. This skill did not come immediately to me. I understood the issues before us; I knew Roberts Rules of Order and meeting procedures, but too often I led with my heart rather than my head on vote counting.

This book is about my experience on Knox County Commission with occasional detours into other events that occurred while I was on commission. I'm likely a curious choice for a tour guide to an atypical local government, but sometimes it is in abnormal moments that the normal is revealed in stark relief. Both become clearer and neither really deserves "normal" in its descriptor ever again. In four years I have passed through a surprise victory, a series of telling vignettes about human behavior when it intersects small amounts of power, a politically motivated shooting at my church, and dozens of colleagues coming and going as our county endured a succession of crises related to attempts to evade term limits and open government.

My time on commission could be seen as a microcosm of dysfunction, or morality play, or a voyage of discovery chock-full of life lessons. The ordering of these experiences works better as a series of subjects, rather than an overlapping and confusing chronology, so let me start by self-introduction.

Mark Harmon, right, with a friend.

1:
Birth of a Political and University Twit

A short, thin young man steps to the microphone at a high school assembly. He has a mop of red hair. His blue eyes are twinkling and he's giving only a tiny hint of sly smile. "I'd like to thank all of you who helped take down my election posters," he says and pauses, "but I wish you had waited until after the election."

The audience erupted in laughter that day in 1974, and I became vice president of my senior class. It was my first electoral success, but it was neither the first nor the last time I would use humor to defuse a situation or to advance an argument.

Pam, Mike and Mark. The Harmon kids in mid-1960s

I grew up in Pittsburgh, the eldest of three kids. Our mom raised us to be courteous, value education, and maintain both self-respect and a sense of humor. Dad was a sport-loving gentle man, a clerk with the gas company and an umpire for local baseball games. We grew up "not poor, just broke," but were in such a loving and upbeat home the tight budgets seemed irrelevant.

We dressed well and spoke properly, making some folks think we were misplaced residents of the wealthy Mount Lebanon suburb rather than denizens of Dormont, an old, brick, working-class borough hard against the southwest border of the city.

We weren't a particularly political family, though there were traces of it. Dinner table conversations sometimes drifted into politics, and kid opinions were discussed and not dismissed. Dad once tried for a seat on the borough council, but didn't get it. I remember a young Democratic congressional candidate, Doug Walgren, bringing his campaign brochures for us to distribute. Election day 1968, the three kids briefly joined Dad outside a polling station—each of us wearing a cardboard letter H, as in HHH or Hubert Horatio Humphrey.

Mom adored John F. Kennedy, and went to see him at a 1960 campaign rally. He was charming, Catholic, and a Navy veteran. Mom, raised in Catholic schools, fell hard. It became a family joke how often she mentioned to me how good I looked in Navy blue.

My first campaign experience came as a fifteen year-old local volunteer with George McGovern's presidential campaign. That campaign ended badly, of course. In my life that meant added ribbing from Kevin Haffics, then a Nixon fan and a fellow student in my homeroom class. In one of life's little ironies I spoke to him four years later just as I started college. He had become a centrist Democrat and a Jimmy Carter supporter.

As best anyone can tell, I was only the second person in three generations of my family to attend college. The first was my cousin Roger. He was the driver on that monumental day when I was dropped off at Penn State. Mom looked tiny and scared as she and Roger rolled away, not saying much for many miles. Separation is tough for a close-knit family, but growth requires challenge and change. We all were up to it, though at times just barely. Less than two months into my college days, my father had the first of many strokes that increasingly would sap his abilities and weaken his health.

University life suited me well. I kept myself busy with classes, speech and debate tournaments, student radio, and opinion columns for the student newspaper. It wasn't long after graduation that I decided my best career choice would be to add a specialized graduate degree. The telecommunications program at Syracuse looked just right. Good scores on the Graduate Record Exam secured a teaching assistantship, revealing a talent and a love for teaching.

Syracuse, in turn, opened doors to an instructor position at Xavier University in Cincinnati. There I had opportunities to pursue good radio journalism. My students picked up some awards in regional journalism competitions. That drew the attention of Ralph Izard, then head of the graduate program at Ohio University. He recruited me to the PhD program, and arranged a teaching assistantship that I could do on a one-year leave from Xavier.

It wasn't easy to teach a full course load while completing additional coursework, comprehensive exams, and a dissertation. Somehow I did it, and there was that delightful day in June 1988 when the family came to Athens, Ohio, to see the doctorate awarded.

Mom hardly could contain herself. I'll remember forever the look on her face when she opened my dissertation and read the dedication to her. She hadn't gone to college; her father's sexist beliefs squelched that dream. That delightful day she oozed love and pride. Grandpa, well he just looked uncomfortable.

Mom and me, the newly minted PhD in 1988.

*Later the image of the degree became a blanket,
a Christmas gift from Becky.*

I'd covered elections frequently during the 1980s, mostly for WVXU-FM, but also helping out on election night 1984 at WBNS in Columbus, Ohio. My political activity during this period, however, was little more than an occasional newspaper column, some assistance for an acquaintance running for Cincinnati City Council, and one memorable clash with politician-turned-anchor (later shock TV host) Jerry Springer, an impromptu debate about journalism and broadcast regulation.

A job offer took me to Texas Tech in Lubbock. I enjoyed the teaching and found favorite places in the community, but politically it was a stark juxtaposition. The area was extremely conservative, deeply nativist, and decidedly Republican. I was a Democratic liberal whose bland Midwest accent still screamed "Yankee" to many.

Nevertheless, buttressed by tenure and continued productivity in my job, I ventured into political and partisan work. I became a precinct chair and later, uncontested, became Lubbock County's Democratic Party Chair. It was around this time that I met over a few drinks, and became fast friends with Molly Ivins, the talented and outrageous columnist with an unerring eye and ear for all things Texan.

Molly once quoted me in a newspaper column as saying that, even though I was running unopposed to be Lubbock County Democratic Party chair, Lubbock had gone so Republican I might have to switch parties to get elected. Of course, I was elected and, in fact, re-elected in a close contest against a friend who I thought was going to run in a local judicial race. Then in 1997-98 I got the crazy notion to run for U.S. Congress.

The car was a powder blue Geo Prizm, the only car I found on both the United Auto Workers American-made list and the Consumer Reports best-buy list. In truth, it was American assembled Toyota parts. It was the politically smart ride for Democrat campaigning for Congress and concerned about U.S. job losses.

When it was damaged by a driver who rear-ended it, I chose another Geo as a replacement, turning down a gas-guzzling, immense truck that I barely could pull myself up to enter. My little car eventually was repaired—in a Lubbock shop appropriately called Body Holly. No, Buddy Holly fans, I did not make that up. No one could. West Texas is what it is.

West Texas towns have a brutal honesty in their names: Plainview, Shallowater, Levelland, Earth, and Brownfield. The long stretches of flat, baked ground are interrupted only sparingly by the pump of a stripper well, a stray group of cattle, or the long, sweeping arm of a cotton irrigation system. Molly Ivins once wrote, "In Lubbock the world is about 88.3 percent sky, which I believe is the correct proportion. It takes a while to get used to, but after you do, Lubbock feels like freedom and everywhere else feels like jail."[2]

The 13th district of Texas in 1998 was a sprawling gerrymandered mess, represented by a lackluster and radical right congressman named Mac Thornberry. The district ran from my little corner of it, east of Avenue Q in Lubbock, all the way up to the northern half of Amarillo. It took in part of the panhandle and all of Wichita Falls, an appendage dropping into parts of Denton on the fringes of the Dallas-Fort Worth metroplex. It was all of 35 counties and part of three more, larger in area than several U. S. states.

I put some 33,000 miles on that tiny car and went through a dozen oil changes during those 14 months campaigning for that seat in Congress. Often in the dark as the little Geo and I would race along the vast emptiness I'd blast music to keep me awake. Janis Joplin, Elvis Costello, the Grateful Dead, the Moody Blues and Meatloaf were the usual fare. Obviously, it wasn't country music and I wasn't in a pick-up truck. Why did I think this would work?

In the morning, however, arising to the morning paper and some orange juice I'd regain my hope and set out on yet another adventure. Those who hate campaigning aren't doing it right. You must bring joy to each encounter and enjoy even the absurd—like the day I campaigned in Mr. Porky's, a biker bar in Denton, Texas. I spread my campaign literature on the green felt of the pool table, assured them I had no interest in advancing mandatory helmet laws (their major concern), and got nods of approval and maybe a few votes when I tore into Washington's corporate welfare as supported by the renting of politicians as needed.

Ah, what could have been.

I had the pleasure of riding in many parades. Once in Pampa I had to jump off a truck designed for transport glass plates, and to whose side I had been clinging. In another town a bump nearly hurled me from a Conestoga wagon. In some parades I would ride in a volunteer's truck bed, too frequently that vehicle would be behind a 12-feet high ceramic bull, the symbol of a local steakhouse. Once I even disco danced, not a recommended sight, behind a local marching band in Denton.

One particularly enthusiastic fan of mine in Wichita Falls kept imploring me to attend events in that area. Some were quite good, but at other times I found myself at the Wildest Pig Cookout with maybe a dozen people, or at the Vernon Burnout, a hot rod and drag racing spectacle that probably was the definition of a non-voter crowd. One 100-degree day several local firefighters and I were the judges at a chili competition. They cleansed their palates with beer. I used grapes and water. I probably just should have gotten drunk. Nearly all the persons attending lived outside the district.

Life on the campaign trail can be tough. Mid-week I'd be attending to my teaching and research duties at Texas Tech, but weekends and summer were on the road, gulping iced tea while waiting for some long-winded local orator to finish the dedication of a park in 100-degree heat.

One particularly weary day I was refueling the car, and a thin disheveled fellow started eyeing my bumper sticker and button. "You running for Congress?" he asked.

"Yes, I am."

"How do you stand on guns?"

"I don't stand on them," I said. "They might go off."

He didn't seem to get it, and wandered away. Perhaps that encounter was in its own way emblematic of the problems of U. S. politics at the end of the 20th century and beginning of the 21st.

Somehow I would win a contested Democratic Primary in which I was outspent, but couldn't quite overcome being outspent 26 to 1 in the general election. The incumbent, of course, ignored me, ignored my challenges to debate, and cruised on all the advantages of the district and incumbency. It was a good feeling, however, that I forced him to spend nearly half a million to beat me, my friends, my message, and my little cruising campaign.

That little car was my trusty steed, my Rocinante in my quixotic tilting at the windmills of West Texas, trying to fill the vast sky with my hopes and dreams. Two months after the campaign ended I took a job at the University of Tennessee in Knoxville, first as a visiting appointment but later becoming a permanent faculty position. I packed the little car and headed east, thinking of the Mac Davis lyric and muttering that happiness truly is Lubbock in a rearview mirror.

2:
Roaring at the Lions Club

The difference between the men and the boys in politics is, and always has been, that the boys want to be something, while the men want to do something.

—Eric Severeid, *CBS News*

"*Maybe* you can beat David Collins," said Madeline Rogero as she donned her coat and headed out my front door. The stress was on the maybe, and her eyes showed much doubt. Madeline was being right and reasonable, of course. She had represented this district on Knox County Commission. She was elected and re-elected against some strong odds. She just recently barely had lost a Knoxville mayoral campaign against the heavily favored establishment candidate, Republican Bill Haslam, millionaire and beneficiary of the Pilot Oil fortune. She proved so impressive that Haslam later called on her to be his community development director.

Rogero was just one of several people sitting around the dining room table that evening. My friend and Knox County Democratic Party chair Jim Gray was encouraging. Another friend and future campaign manager Paul Witt stood ready to crunch numbers on what was possible. City Councilman Bob Becker, who I'd help with media during his successful run, shared Madeline's doubts. Lizajean Holt knew me well from our days in 2002. We were part of the Jim Andrews team, an energetic band that ran a great campaign and nearly beat an incumbent sheriff who had to summon all the advantages of power, money, and party just to survive. Lizajean said yes; she thought I could do it.

There were two options on the table. I could run against Billy Tindell in the Democratic Primary. He had the advantage of 36 years on commission and the name recognition that goes with such longevity. It would have been a short campaign, could prove divisive, and might invite the Republicans to field a candidate for the general election.

The more logical choice was to challenge the Republican in the other second district seat. He was somewhat popular in his eight years and had served a stint as the commission chair, but the longer time period until the August election would give me time to win the only way this could be won, a grassroots assault largely under the radar of both media and Collins.

Actually it was time for both Tindell and Collins to go. Both had been there up to or well beyond the eight-year term limit imposed by the voters. That limit should have kicked in this election cycle, but that matter had been finessed locally so it wouldn't apply, a charade that later would collapse. Nevertheless, I knew a term-limits message alone would not be sufficient. I began to craft a message around the three S's: schools (not enough support from county), sprawl (unsustainable and costly), and sheriff (too much wasteful empire building).

All these themes had a successful test run during a primary election candidate forum at the Fountain City Lions Club. A small portion of the second district was in Fountain City. David Collins and I both were there, as were a gaggle of Republicans fighting for two seventh district seats and grumbling at each other. Quickly I discovered a surprise kindred spirit, a neighborhood-friendly, sprawl-hating farmer named James McMillan, running a long-shot bid in the seventh.

News anchor Robin Wilhoit moderated the forum, but the organizers created the questions and made them known to the candidates in advance. The answers thus were largely canned, but on the spot I improvised a few things that worked quite well.

One question asked whether you considered yourself a guardian of current ways, one who tinkers with modest revisions, or a change agent. Most candidates said one or the other, or even a combination. I said I was a hell raiser. That drew some laughs and even some tepid applause.

The planned questions that night also had one about what you had learned from your experiences in office. It was a question that favored incumbents, so I had planned a novel reply. I talked about my days on the University of Tennessee Faculty Senate, fighting unsuccessfully for an end to tobacco product sales on campus, but settling for a resolution—wholeheartedly supported by Chancellor Loren Crabtree—for smoking-free entrances to campus buildings. The resolution passed; all of us had a reprieve from ducking a carcinogenic cloud on our way to offices and classrooms. No sooner had it passed, however, than one UT vice president sent crews out to bolt large standing ashtrays into the cement by entrances. "I could have gone into hell-raiser mode," I told the forum crowd, "but instead I went to the chancellor's open forum and joked with him about it. The next week the ashtray tops were screwed off, and in their place were signs reading Smoke-Free Entrance."

I stood out that night in several ways—the only Democrat, the only one not in a dark suit (Becky picked out a nice tan suit), the only one who would have known the hell-raiser line came from Mother Jones, and likely the only one who knew who Mother Jones was or had read the magazine named after her.

"I'm going to do something rarely heard at these events," I said at one late moment in the meeting, "I'm going to say something nice about my opponent. David Collins has done some good things on commission in his eight years there. I thank him, but it's time in the spirit of term limits to bring in news ideas. I'm running not just on term limits, but also what you might call the Three S's..."

Collins responded, "Thanks, uh, Mark."

After the formal session reporter Betty Bean put questions to James McMillan and me. Which projects did we oppose and why? We both answered the proposed (and wasteful, destructive, and unneeded) business park called Midway Road. Any others? We'll take the new ones as they come up. She looked dubious, and neither of us could match her knowledge of process and players. We both tried to persuade her that we were quick learners, guided by good principles. Much later I would earn a nod of approval from her.

Later I'd learn from Jim Gray that he had a friend that night in the audience. He confided to Jim that he had no idea who I was before the event, but left that night as someone leaning toward being a Mark Harmon fan.

3:
Two-a-Day Drills, Two-fers, and Too Much

Becky at our table during the Knox County Democratic Party's Truman Day.

Some longtime Knox Democrats cling to the philosophy and phrase "When Democrats vote, Democrats win." No, not really, especially in this area. The political graveyard is full of well-intentioned people who thought they possessed some mystical power to get long dormant, and presumably Democratic-leaning, persons to vote. Paul Witt and I avoided that temptation, instead relying on ideas taught by Democracy For Tennessee, the successor organization to Howard Dean's presidential campaign. We'd also rely on ideas gleaned from academic study of campaigns, *Campaigns & Elections* magazine, and from campaign practitioner seminars shown on C-SPAN. Nerdy, yes, but also amazingly effective.

Precinct-by-precinct Paul and I analyzed voting behavior in similar and recent primaries. We looked at Solid Democrats, Solid Republicans, Leaning Democrats, and Leaning Republicans—all based on public records of party primary selection. We knew the key would be the "leans," especially those leaning Republican. The math was simple. Every time I get someone not likely to vote to show up and vote or me, that's a "one," one more vote for me. Every time I get a regular voter to opt for me instead of my opponent that's a "two," one less vote for my opponent and one more vote for me. Ones are valuable; twos are twice as valuable.

The academic research about block walking suggested that a candidate gets one extra vote for every twelve of the targeted homes visited. You never know which one of the twelve until you do the work. Personal contact is much more valuable than mass media, but some media, at least some direct mail post cards, would be necessary as well.

So that was the plan, shoe leather. Paul wrote down a number on what percentage he thought I could get if it all worked perfectly. I set about preparing lists of streets, highlighting the homes of frequent voters, visiting all but the Solid R's, adjusting as necessary in the field, and talking to all out in their yards or passing me on the sidewalk.

In the hallway of our house Becky let me post a giant map of the Second District. I'd use different highlighter pens to color a street when I had finished it. The map was not only an organizational tool, but also an inspiration to show me where I must go next. I'd work heavily senior streets in mid-morning, come home for some relief, and then do other streets in the late afternoons and early evenings. These were my summer two-a-days. Becky would pack a cooler with a wet washcloth and bottled water. I'd pick up some peach tea at Sonic, and keep pushing myself to walk blocks.[3]

None of this might have mattered had David Collins not given me a great tool for each personal contact. Perhaps he was too confident of success or perhaps he genuinely believed the tortured logic, but he joined a lawsuit whose effect would be to invalidate the county charter so he could stay on the ballot.

The background story is incredibly convoluted, but here is a condensed timeline. Voters put in our county charter a term limit provision. Long-time office holders didn't like that provision and chose to stress a state attorney general's opinion that charter governments could not impose term limits. Advisory opinions from the state attorney general are rather weak. The first court to tackle the same issue holds greater precedent. Locally, however, the power brokers liked the opinion, looked no further, and treated it as binding law. When the matter finally got to the courts, via a Memphis case, the term limits prevailed.

That should have been the end of it, but a local judge loudly hinted that he would entertain the argument that the local charter was so flawed it was invalid. The local pols got the hint, and put an item before the same judge so—voila—the charter was void and with it the term limits. All of the efforts of write-in candidates as last-minute primary challengers and other responses to the Memphis ruling largely were for naught.

The lawsuit to invalidate the charter had been brought by five long-time commissioners, including both Tindell and Collins. Thus, I could go to every door and say, "David's a good guy, but he never should have sued to wipe out our charter, just so he could ignore term limits." So I did.

The court ruling from Memphis validating term limits for charter counties came too late to change the primary ballot. A friend of mine, Amy Broyles, secured the most primary write-in votes to replace Tindell. In fact, the total number of write-in votes exceeded the vote total for Tindell, the only on-ballot candidate. The local court ruling effectively put that aside, and kept Billy Tindell on the general election ballot thanks to his slim plurality. Amy bravely ventured on with a general election write-in campaign as an independent. Tindell faced no Republican or other on-ballot opposition, but Amy secured nearly 30% of the vote as a write-in, despite heavy party regular blowback for her valiant and ethical stand against the local ploy. We became something of a ticket, allies and friends fighting the insider game being played.

Amy and I picked up a statewide endorsement from our progressive friends at Democracy for Tennessee.

Crashing the Commission 29

Scenes from Amy Broyles' write-in announcement: Becky Harmon and Jamie Parkey make balloon animals. Aidyn Parkey gets a ride, Amy speaks out, Avery Parkey naps, supporters smile.

In fact, there was a more formal outrage ticket, the Orange Ballot. It was a collection of candidates supporting term limits and giving voice to the outrage against the insider game. The Orange Ballot group mostly was Democrats, but included Amy's independent candidacy and even one Republican, an unusual used car salesman named Greg "Lumpy" Lambert who said he supported term limits and whose political experience previously consisted of appearing in tax protest before County Commission in costume with a giant screw appearing to impale his large torso.

The voters of Knox County may well have been outraged by the legal shenanigans, but apparently weren't willing to cross parties to express that anger. The local daily newspaper, the *Knoxville News Sentinel*, mostly was willing to put aside its Republican leanings and endorse change. The paper endorsed the challengers against the "gang of five" who filed the charter-nullifying lawsuit. All of the challengers, that is, except one. The paper opted for Collins.[4]

Caption Contest Winner

The Knoxville News Sentinel did a story on my opponent's web site, but not mine. What a shame. At the close of the campaign you would have found on my election blog this actual quote from my opponent at an Oakwood-Lincoln Park Neighborhood Association meeting.

Election Day is always a volatile mix of anxiety, energy, exhaustion, and relief. County elections in Tennessee fall on the first Thursday of August. In 2006 this was a sweltering day with a threat of downpours. I worked the largest voting precinct, Inskip Elementary, a key area where I knew I had to minimize Collins' margin. Becky worked our home precinct. Paul and Amy each were at another large and important precincts, as were my "iron man and iron woman," Dan and Linda Haney. Volunteers kept shifts at other polling locations. We also unveiled large sandwich boards reminding voters of what Collins and Tindell did in the term-limits mischief.

Something about the shared ordeal of grueling 8 a.m. to 8 p.m. shift at the polling place unites even opposing candidates. Umbrellas, spray bottles, newspapers, snacks, and drinks all are offered and shared. Volunteers from differing sides talk about family, weather, sports, and other innocuous subjects.

I sprayed some mist on Billy Tindell. David Collins' son was friendly enough, even as he seemed to keep himself in a voter sight line to block the view of the sandwich boards. The only conflict arose when Karen Collins took objection to something I said to a voter. "You're going to lose," she blurted. "You're an embarrassment. Every time you go out campaigning, we get calls and more supporters." My guess is she would take a loss harder than David would. That's a shame. It never was personal, just a different view on how things should be.

That night the Orange Ballot candidates and friends gathered at Shonos, a restaurant and bar on Market Square. The returns came in quickly and badly. Our great candidates were going down in defeat, many by large margins. My friend Jim Andrews lost his bid for a judicial position, as did my friend Ken Irvine. People milled about. Some gave news interviews. Some exchanged small talk. Then District Two results popped up on the television screens. I was winning. I pumped my fist in the air and yelled, "Yes!" I really couldn't hear the sound on the news coverage, but clearly something about a big upset was being said. I hugged Becky. I hugged Paul. I hugged Jim Gray.

One radio interviewer said, "Well, you're the man of the hour."

"Yes, I suppose so," I said. "I just wish some of my friends were going along for the ride." Indeed, the final tally for District Two, Seat A, was 1882 votes for Harmon, 1688 for Collins. I won with 54.25% of the vote. Paul's "everything right" projection was 54.37%. On occasion I still ask him what happened to that missing twelve-hundredths of a percent.

Campaign Manager Paul Witt celebrates with me on Election Night, August 2006.

Jim Andrews shook my hand. "I'm so proud of you, boy. Your win almost makes all this other nonsense worth it, though I still don't know why you want to hang around with that gang of thieves."

The only other Orange Ballot candidate who won was, gulp, Lumpy?!⁵

The next morning I read in the *News Sentinel* a quote from David Collins to his supporters. "To be honest with you, I didn't see it coming," he said.⁶

I remembered a time when we both had attended a meeting of the Alice Bell Spring Hill Neighborhood Association. The speaker was grateful that his topic was significant enough to warrant the attendance of the commissioner. "And the next commissioner," I interjected. "Yah, right." David muttered under his breath but just loud enough for me to hear. "Yah, right," I thought that post-election morning. "Yah, right."

The August 2006 commission meeting was a lame-duck session, taking place after the election but before the new group was sworn in. The commissioners took up the proposed Midway Business Park. I sat in the audience and watched the neighborhood groups present a compelling case complete with expert testimony: The business park model is too restrictive and narrow. The plan violates past agreements with the neighborhoods. The karst geography (sinkholes) makes the proposed park problematic. The current half-empty business parks are sufficient. All the Chamber of Commerce and Development Corporation could do was repeat bland generalities about growth. The Commission majority, including my opponent, sided with sprawl, the Chamber, and the poor plan. I remembered why I ran. It was a weird, illogical, compromised and petty world I would be entering. It may be too much to change. But the effort was needed, the tasks were needed, and the forthcoming lessons in human nature and organizational behavior would be worth the ride.

Knox County Commission as of January 2007.

Photo by Jon Gustin.

4:
God, Gays, Guns, and Goofy Government

An honest politician is regarded as a sort of marvel, comparable a calf with five legs, and the news that one has appeared is commonly received with derision.

—Henry Louis Mencken,
The American Language (1945), p. 282.[7]

Knox County Mayor Mike Ragsdale arranged a religious ceremony to precede the oath taking by all of us elected in 2006. Becky and I attended, baffled equally by the parking arrangements, passes, and protocol. The ceremony was in a downtown Episcopal Church. I remembered Molly Ivins' line about Episcopalians being genetically Republican,[8] or my retort that you know you're in the Deep South when even the Episcopalians handle snakes.

For comfort I brought along my Unitarian Universalist minister, Chris Buice. His father and brother both are Episcopal ministers, so he speaks the lingo and could translate for me. He also could hear any of my whispered jokes following the priest, rabbi, and minister homilies.

The swearing-in itself in the Large Assembly Room of the City County Building went smoothly. All of us new commissioners were sworn in bulk, no speeches. I felt the need to be holding a copy of the Jefferson Bible, the volume edited by the third president to emphasize the philosophy and spirituality of Jesus, not miracles or mythologies. It had been given to me and signed by Chris Buice for the occasion. I still have and treasure it.

There's a picture of me looking fairly somber, and Becky smiling as I raised my hand. It was a big moment for all of us new folks, but one could observe it was really a celebration of the power bases, mayor and sheriff, and the personal fiefdoms of long-time elected lesser players like the clerk, trustee, and register of deeds.

Sheriffs in Tennessee historically and functionally exercise a significant amount of power. They have a Peace Officer Standards and Training Commission that can and has been wielded on the credentials of candidates, notably challengers, in attempts to get such candidates off the ballot. State legislation protects sheriff budgets from cuts. The worst they can get each budget year is the same as last year.

How big was the split between the Knox County mayor and sheriff? They had separate welcoming events in the fall of 2006 for the commissioners. Mayor Ragsdale had a boxed lunch in the Small Assembly Room with some aides and department heads handy to answer questions. Sheriff Tim Hutchison had the group for buffet lunch in his inner sanctum, a meeting room and kitchen area with several built-in TV monitors. As we exited his control room, he reminded us of the security protection. If we tried to get lunch there in future days, we'd likely be arrested. Laughter abounds from the commissioner veterans, but I found the whole thing vaguely disconcerting.

"What do you want?" That's what Mayor Mike Ragsdale and his top aide Mike Arms asked to start their individual meeting with me. I was taken aback and stumbled around mentioning everything from policies discouraging sprawl to grants for making healthy locally grown food available to school cafeterias. The latter idea I borrowed from Morgan Spurlock, the fellow behind *Supersize Me*.

I probably came across as naïve and idealistic. Heck, I was naïve and idealistic, and in some ways still may be. I suppose a veteran of local politics might have secured guarantees of a park or library, then go-along-to-get-along with a wink and a nod.

People who study leadership sometimes write about transactional versus transformational techniques. Transactional is the implied deal—what you give in expectation for what you get. Transformational is more difficult and requires much more consultation and communication. It involves inspiring people to develop a shared set of goals, and motivating them by trust, patience, and a sense of involvement toward task completion.[9]

Some of both may be necessary, but in retrospect the balance in Knox County clearly was out of whack. It was almost all transactional, not only commission but also the little fiefdoms of fee offices, including an excessively powerful sheriff running not only his area, but exercising power elsewhere as well. Careful observers also would see developers who double as contributors getting nearly all what they want. In short, the proclamations, public speeches, events, hearings, and meetings were for show; the votes were for dough. The usual shorthand for all this was the "courthouse mentality."

My meeting with Arms and Ragsdale ended with the mayor pointing out his signed photo with Governor Phil Bredesen. Ragsdale talked about how it showed he could work with Democrats. I told Ragsdale I probably could get him a signed photo of Dennis Kucinich. He laughed. I grinned, all the while thinking that established order was in such a different place it couldn't even see where I was. How could I survive and thrive in the current encrusted model?

The quickest and least controversial items on commission agendas tend to be "pass through money," routine approvals of various federal and state grants sought and obtained by county departments. The sheriff perhaps gets a grant for new radio equipment, or the health department gets a grant for child immunizations. One meeting, however, an unexpected flare-up came from one of these routine matters.

Political humorist Scott McNutt, author of the "Snark Bites" column in the News Sentinel, tends to refer to Commissioner R. Larry Smith as Our Larry. Our Larry, former Republican chair, pulled from the consent agenda a routine health grant for HIV treatment. He then went into a fiery blurt, expressing his revulsion at "men having sex with men."

The grant still passed, but a few other commissioners apparently were willing to turn down the federal money to address this matter just to join Smith's sentiment. In a later, quieter portion of the meeting I reminded all that we were fighting a disease, not expressing views about one means of transmission. Allison Wagley, a mayoral aide who I'd worked with on a Magnet Schools Task Force, later thanked me for bringing things back to a reasoned tone.

Only on a few occasions did Knox County Commission drift into the murky waters of national developments. Lumpy felt compelled to offer up a resolution honoring Charlton Heston shortly after the death of the actor and former National Rifle Association president. After a bit of banter we gave Lumpy what he wanted, but then the practical matter arose of what do you do with the actual proclamation? We eventually gave Lumpy the Heston proclamation and let Lambert do any next steps.

It was easier to complete the task when twice I had us honor the Knoxville Ice Bears for winning the Southern Professional Hockey League Championship. I turned and handed the proclamations to the coach and manager; I even held aloft the trophy.

Today, I am a hockey player.

Photos by Jon Gustin.

The only time I ventured close to any national or international concerns was a modest response to the genocide in Darfur. I persuaded the commission to pass a resolution urging a Finance Director and Pension Board to review our investments to see if we had any Sudanese investments we could divest. Pension Board, Commissioner Ivan Harmon's turf, sent me a mind-your-own-business note. Finance Director John Troyer was more willing to look. There likely wasn't anything to find, but I'm not sure he ever reviewed the items.

In light of our nod to the cinematic Moses, it shouldn't be surprising Knox County Commission also felt compelled to weigh in on matters of God. The previously mentioned Ivan Harmon, no relation, is a long-time political good-ol'-boy, serving stints on a school board, city council, and commission. Normally he sits quietly in meetings, reliably voting the opposite of my position on almost all controversial matters.

Ivan, however, decided that we should revisit a matter on which he had been rebuffed previously. It was a boilerplate radical right resolution, a bit of historical revisionism calling on all levels of government to publicly recognize God as the foundation of our national heritage. I suggested that the public was sufficiently intelligent to come to its own understanding of this matter without any guidance from the Knox County Commission.

Others picked up the obvious snub to the establishment clause in the First Amendment. I was particularly proud of one eloquent woman from the audience who spoke to commission. She spoke about Article Six of the U. S. Constitution "no religious Test shall ever be required as a Qualification to any Office or public Trust under the United States." She quoted from the 1797 Treaty of Tripoli that "the government of the United States of America is not, in any sense, founded on the Christian religion." Ivan, however, was in full fervor and would not be deterred. He waved a dollar bill, bellowing the "In God We Trust" on the back. Personally I thought the mixing of God and Mammon didn't work for him. Thomas "Tank" Strickland, normally a quiet member of commission, chastised Ivan for revisiting this divisive item blurring separation of church and state, but the resolution passed 8-3 (we were down to eleven seats because of the voiding of the Black Wednesday appointments).[10]

Another big advocate for the God resolution was Lumpy. Of all the characters on commission he is one who deserves special attention. Greg "Lumpy" Lambert's previously noted giant screw costume was a protest against Mayor Mike Ragsdale's proposed wheel tax, a development that became a perpetual complaint of those opposed to Ragsdale and a lingering rift among the local Republicans.

Lumpy and guns have a long, heavily publicized history. He gained attention for giving away a gun with every purchase at his used car lot. Lumpy once pulled a gun on an attempted car thief, one who later was found to have killed someone. One Lumpy campaign stunt was a fundraiser in an armory. Our then county Democratic chair, Jim Gray, attended on a lark, and won the gun door prize.

One of the more unusual powers of a county commissioner is to sign marriage certificates. I only did so once, officiating for a lovely couple of UT staffers who wanted to marry and square away their work benefits before their formal family ceremony. The secretaries in the School of Journalism and Electronic Media were surprised that day to see me reading to a couple their vows and also quoting from a reading used in the ceremony for Becky and me. Lumpy's methods are different. One February 14th, Valentine's Day, Lumpy offered a "shotgun wedding" special at the armory. No one took him up on the offer. Maybe the sentiment, or an official nicknamed Lumpy, scared off nuptial couples. He did, however, renew the vows of one couple as they all gathered in the studio and on the air of a local radio program.[11]

Several times I heard Lumpy compare county commission to high school—replete with cliques and an "in" crowd. The fact he viewed it that way is quite revealing. Lumpy desperately wanted to be part of the "in" crowd, and to him that means outside the Knoxville city limits, not inside; sheriff loving and mayor hating, Republican not Democratic (or Democrat, no "ic" in the local parlance). It meant former chairman Scott "Scoobie" Moore, Ivan, and Lumpy's fellow used car salesman Paul Pinkston.

I've certainly fallen short of the standard sometimes, but I try to judge actions not people. Lumpy needed friends; he may have been looking for them in the wrong place. He tried to invite other commissioners to an island vacation. He made videos; I remember one with a pirate theme and a fake parrot. Less intriguing television would be the couple of times we appeared together on cable access programs. More intriguing television would be the commission moments when Lumpy got so upset he left his chair to challenge someone in the audience or speaking at the lectern.[12] Lumpy's behavior disrupted two routine community meeting of the Task Force on Ridge, Slope and Hillside Development. At Karns Community Center he attempted to take over the meeting. The remaining commissioners felt the need to say "enough" and formally censured him.[13]

5:
Molly Ivins and Black Wednesday

Nobody has a more sacred obligation to obey the law than those who make the law.
—Sophocles, Greek poet, 496-406 B. C. E.

I met Molly Ivins in early 1994, and for reasons that will become clear later I prefer to view the bizarre political machinations of Knox County's scandalous Black Wednesday through the prism of Molly's big-as-Texas heart and life.

Molly had come to Lubbock, Texas, for an opening event at the Godbold Cultural Center. She always had a soft spot for the Society of Professional Journalists, so she also had arranged some events for the local chapter.

For those who didn't know Molly, you missed an interaction with a force of nature as powerful as a West Texas tornado. She reported from many places, but this gifted writer was at her best piercing the pomposity and exposing the foibles of Texas politics. *Molly Ivins Can't Say That, Can She?* her collection of columns, was a must read among the people I worked with in both newsrooms and academia.

My friend and the anchor for whom I wrote copy, Katie Keifer, felt compelled to read certain sections aloud. She had to stop frequently to catch her breath from being bent over in laughter.

By the time of Molly's visit I had given up working as a TV news producer, and now devoted my spare time to politics. As the line of autograph-seekers wound round itself, I leaned toward Molly's ear and whispered, "I have a John Henry story to tell you."

She lit up and replied, "You just pull up a chair and sit here beside me." John Henry Faulk was a folksy radio performer who in the 1950s ran afoul of the Red Scare crowd. He was blacklisted, but beat the blacklisters in court. He spent much of the remainder of his often-hard life speaking out for the preciousness and importance of the Bill of Rights. He and Molly often found themselves paired to do battle against assorted censors, charlatans, and book banners.

My story wasn't much, just about meeting Faulk when he spoke at Syracuse and had some choice comments about the timidity evident in network TV newscasts. Molly and I later gabbed politics over some beers. She later wrote in my copy of her book, "For Mark Harmon who stands tall among the tens of liberals to be found in Lubbock. Raise more hell! And keep laughin' too. With many thanks for your help and all best wishes in your frontline freedom-fightin'!"

Molly's next column on the many reasons she loved Lubbock mentioned me in passing, and the line also showed up in her next book; it even was clipped and quoted in an American Airlines review of the book. Friends tore out the magazine page and mailed it to me.

The next Texas Democratic Convention Molly came running up to the Lubbock delegation and bellowed, "Where's Mark?" They explained that unfortunately I was quite ill and unable to attend. We exchanged some calls but didn't meet again until two years later at the State Democratic Convention in Austin. Molly was in her element along Austin's raucous Sixth Street, laughing, talking politics, and sharing a meal and drinks with a dozen folks.

We kept in touch only sporadically during my 1998 run for Congress, and the beginnings of my adventures in East Tennessee. She had written in her column, at first incidentally and later in detail, about her cancer diagnosis and her treatment. I told her of the women I'd known who had beaten cancer and told her she had no option but to do the same. I hadn't yet taken the opportunity in January 2007 to write her on my Knox County Commissioner stationery. She would have been amused that it was authentic, and astounded about how it all came to be.

The past is prologue, and the prologue necessary to understand Black Wednesday begins with November 8, 1994, the day Knox County voters approved by a three-to-one margin term limits for most elected county offices. The voter intent was clear and compelling, the affected elected officials would be limited to two consecutive terms. The term limits would apply to the county mayor/executive, county commissioners, sheriff, trustee, register of deeds, clerk, and property assessor.

By February of 1995, however, local office holders looking for an excuse to avoid term limits had one. Tennessee's Attorney General offered the opinion that term limits, despite the expanded local rule of charter government, could not be applied to offices stated in the state constitution. As far as strength of judicial authority goes, an opinion from the Attorney General is about as low on the chain of authority as one can get. The first court of any jurisdiction that rules on the matter has greater precedent. The local fiefdoms of power had the answer they wanted in the proffered opinion and preferred to stop asking the question.

The question nevertheless was asked, but at the opposite end of the state. Voters in Shelby County, home to Memphis, approved a very similar term limits provision. As March 2006 came to a close, the Tennessee Supreme Court upheld term limits in Shelby County, and by precedent Knox County as well. Pandemonium broke loose at our city-county building and in related offices and political circles. Was it too late to remove term-limited names from the May primary ballots? Yes, according to that state election coordinator. What happens in that case? Political parties would meet and by their own procedures pick a ballot replacement, similar to the circumstances if a nominee died.

The stultifying effect of ignored term limits almost immediately became apparent. Record numbers of people, many perhaps previously deterred by the Herculean task of challenging an incumbent, declared themselves as write-in candidates. The internal mechanisms of party meetings and procedures, normally lightly attended and often fairly dull, rose suddenly in interest and significance. This burst of grassroots democracy and the Supreme Court ruling momentarily had the political establishment reeling. The insiders, however, were not done. Another term limits avoidance mechanism soon emerged.

A local judge, Chancellor John Weaver, had hinted broadly that there could be something wrong with the charter in which term limits resided. Five term-limited commissioners got the hint. All of them in their oath of office had sworn to uphold the county charter. Nevertheless, Diane Jordan, David Collins, Billy Tindell, Phil Guthe, and John Greiss would go to Weaver's court challenging the charter. That case was still being decided when May 2, 2006, rolled around—primary election day and my 49th birthday. Three term-limited commissioners lost, but nine survived to go onto the general election. Billy Tindell barely survived. More write-in votes were cast against him than on-ballot votes for him, but the write-ins were split—two-thirds for Amy Broyles, a third for Jonathan Wimmer. Amy would take on the immensely more difficult challenge of a write-in for the general election, facing an entrenched incumbent who would use all the mechanisms of power to cling to power.

Weaver's decision came down on June 9, 2006. He declared the charter "incomplete, invalid and ineffective" plus not properly filed with Tennessee. So this tissue-thin excuse to keep the term-limited on the ballot will hold until the August county general election. Eight of the nine term-limited win. My victory over David Collins is the only exception. On reflection it was clear that while voters were upset about term limits being ignored, they largely weren't ready to cross party lines to express that anger.

Pandemonium soon would break loose at the courthouse again. The date was January 12, 2007, the day the Tennessee Supreme Court ruled the Knox County Charter despite flaws is valid. County Commission would have to appoint replacements for the eight commissioners and four fee officers who must leave.[14]

Mayor Ragsdale held a news conference. Initially he talked about the remaining eleven members of commission and how they should proceed to fill the vacancies. He was pleased the Court upheld the charter, called term limits "the will of the people," and expressed mixed emotions because people with whom he had served would be leaving. Mainly it was a generic and general call for open process and careful consideration. Opposing views quickly and surprisingly came forward. Law Director John Owings said the ousted commissioners possibly could vote on their successors. He eventually would craft an argument that because the Court allowed the ousted to serve until their replacements were named (presumably to avoid problems in fee offices, and specifically "to assure the continuation of essential government services") that allowed the ousted commissioners to continue to vote on all matters, including successors. Commission Chair Scott Moore blustered that any procedural choices were those of the commission, and not the mayor.[15] The old sheriff/mayor split was kicking into a higher gear.

The choices then made in mid-January 2007 would play out in the train wreck the occurred on the last day of the month. The regular commission meeting that month was astounding for its lack of concern about the public will and open process. Would we ask the state legislature for special legislation to allow a special election? No, that proposal went down, 14-5. Would we follow my alternate proposal—using the early voting sites to create a non-binding plebiscite to learn the public will before we voted on replacements? No. Only Commissioner John Schmid voted with me for that idea. Would we hold open hearings so replacement candidates could state their case to commissioners and public alike? No. John Owings told us the law was silent on that matter. We probably could. We didn't have to.[16] The majority chose not to. So now the locomotive was at top speed, the rails were warped, and the ties were weak.

Chairman Scott Moore cobbled together a list of commissioners for a special meeting the morning of January 31st. My name appears on that list only because of a communication error with a commission secretary. I thought she was asking if I was available on that date. I was, but didn't support the holding of the meeting as she thought. It turned out to be a miscommunication of little matter. Scoobie had more than enough names to rush through his method of naming replacements.

Some of us tried to improvise some public process on our own. Commissioners Mike Hammond and Craig Leuthold put together an event for replacement candidates at the Cedar Bluff Library meeting room.[17] It was packed, standing room only.

Becky helped me pull together a meeting to be held in the Second District, but covering all offices affected. Originally it was to be held at Fulton High School, but the school rather late discovered it had a conflict. I quickly found an alternate site, Whittle Springs Middle School auditorium. The only lingering problem from the switch was monitoring local news organizations. Even though the newsrooms had been informed of the location change several times, a couple times I had to call TV news producers while newscasts were in progress to secure a quick correction.

More than 200 people showed up for the forum. The thirteen commissioners who attended were invited to sit on the stage and take notes. Several did, but some chose to remain in the audience or the back of the room, sometimes stepping out to chat in the foyer. Becky greeted all arrivals, and the biggest round of applause was when I thanked her.

I followed the same procedure for all contests, one I announced in advance on several neighborhood listservs and the blog Knoxviews: three-minute speeches from candidates followed by audience questions. For the second district and countywide seats we went in alphabetical order. When I called the other districts to the stage, they sorted themselves out as to who went first, etc. The timekeeper was a volunteer with the League of Women Voters. Generally candidates kept to the time. Only three times did I ask anyone to wrap up—and in each case the timekeeper "Stop" card had been up and swinging.

Two volunteers from the mayor's office helped me identify raised hands during the early Q&A periods. This became unnecessary as the forum progressed. The questions were few, but generally direct and revealing. We shortened the time to minute-and-a-half speeches for the other districts, and still just barely kept the forum under three hours in length.

I also decided to do a forum preference poll. No one had advance notice of my intent to do this. The only clue to anyone was my very open advocacy for a non-binding referendum as a way to squeeze greater public input into commission's process. A commission secretary helped me photocopy it, between 3:30 and 3:45 the day of the forum. I still wasn't certain I'd use it, but when the forum began it looked like I had just enough volunteers to distribute it so I decided to do so. Two volunteers with LWV tallied the results at the end of the forum. I sent those results to this blog, several listservs, and news organizations—all with stated cautions about the reliability and value of the measure, and noting that other factors such as candidate qualifications and quality of responses should play a role in decision making.

Most respondents were from the second district; most followed the directions to indicate a preference only in their own district and the countywide offices. Some did mark in more than one commission district, accounting for an overall number that initially seems larger than the attendance (if one were to add all votes cast for commission candidates together, as one sharp-eyed blogger apparently did).

Those tallies were as follows:

Sheriff Candidates

Randy Tyree, 83; JJ Jones, 24; Isa Infante, 6; J. Lee Tramel, 3; 1 vote each for Eric Beals, and write-ins Bobby Waggoner and Jim Andrews.

Trustee Candidates

Fred Sisk, 54; Jeannie Mathews, 19.

Register of Deeds Candidates

Scott Emge, 58; Sherry Witt, 30; Arrison Kirby, 15; 1 write in for Bill Waters.

County Clerk Candidates

Billy Tindell, 39; George Stooksbury, 38; Carolyn Carter Jensen, 26; 12 write-in votes for Kelvin Moxley, 5 for Jim Andrews; and 1 for Michael Paseur.

District 1 Commission Candidates

Nick Della Volpe, 23; Helen Diane Lewis, 10; Evelyn Gill and Josh Jordan, 9 each; Leslie Terry, 5; Robert Minter, 4; Ann Dingus, 2; and 1 each for Jewel Cason, Rubye Wright, and Pete Drew

District 2 Commission Candidates

Amy Broyles, 62: Jonathan Wimmer, 31; Cortney Piper, 21; Joseph L. Williams, 8; Deborah Porter, 6; Bruce White, 3: Steve Roberts, 2; write-in for Greg McKay, 1; Charles Bolus, 0.

District 4 Commission Candidates (two seats)

Elaine Davis, 42; Ed Shouse and Joan Wagner, 10 each; Scott Davis, 8; Lee Tramel, 6; William Daniels and Richard Cate, 5 each; Debbie Barton, 3; Mike Alford, Archie Ellis and Lisa Bogaty, 2 each, Craig Fisher, 1; James Smelcher, 0.

District 5 Commission Candidates

Tom Salter, 35; Brian Hornback, 6; Robin Butler, 3; Tamara Boyer, Kyle Philips, and Gregory Harrison, 2 each; 1 for Teresa Shupp; 0 votes for Marilyn Cobble, Ken Gross, or Pamela Treacy.

District 6 Commission Candidates

Sharon Cawood, 23; Charles Giles and Jimmie Shelton, 8 each; Justin Wiseman and Roger Hyman, 2 each; 1 write-in for Kelvin Moxley; Randy Williams, 0.

District 8 Commission Candidates

Jack Huddleston, 10; Kay Frazier and Tom Pressley, 7 each; Jim Eubanks, 6; Maurice Freed, 4; Doug Dawkins and Gary Koontz, 2 each; Teresa Clapp, 1; 1 write-in for Gary Sellers; George Carney, 0.

District 9 Commission Candidates

Joshua Lowe, 8; Matthew Myers, 7; Rob Huddleston and Gary Underwood, 4 each; Randy Hinton, 3; Bob Norton, 2; 1 each for write-ins Steve McGill, Bruce Hill, Martin Pleasant, and Mike Leventhal; Chuck Ward, 0.[18]

I clung to a hope that at the forthcoming meeting perhaps some unlikely alliances might form. Perhaps even some unplanned commissioner public discussion. I remembered Molly Ivins' stories about the late Houston-area congressman Mickey Leland. When Leland was in the Texas Legislature he was as shrewd as he was self-deprecating. He surprised the liberal-labor coalition when that group took the Black Caucus for granted. He threw Black Caucus support to a West Texas redneck named Billy Wayne Clayton in exchange for the clout of several committee chairmanships. Molly wrote, "Leland came out of the meeting with Clayton waving a tiny Confederate flag and announced, 'We done sold de plantation'."[19]

I wasn't looking to pull a Mickey Leland deal or compromise, nor was I supporting the backroom politics that earns the Texas legislature the moniker The Best Little Statehouse in Texas. I was hoping against hope that it wasn't going to be a train wreck of sullen self-interest and clashing power blocs —that instead we'd see moments of persuasion sprinkled with some public give and take. Nope.

"It's going to be Bolus." That's what Lumpy said to me via my cell phone, as Becky and I drove to the meeting. I was incredulous. There were eight announced candidates for the second district position. Seven showed up at the Whittle Springs forum; all did well. Charles Bolus was the one candidate who did not show or participate in much public process. He had a rather thin resume beyond his assistant principal duties at Gresham Middle. I later was told he was co-treasurer of Chairman Scott Moore's campaign. Lumpy's call was another bad omen of what was percolating.

Some 400 people crowded the Large Assembly Room of the City County Building that morning of January 31, 2007. The appointments would take three hours and 27 minutes, but not without showing the public a circus of intrigues, recesses, anger, and power plays.[20] The appointments would start with the countywide offices. Those passed rather easily. Sheriff Tim Hutchison's top deputy J. J. Jones overwhelmingly was selected to take over as sheriff. Top assistants Fred Sisk and Sherry Witt took over respectively in the Trustee and Register of Deeds Offices. A few of us preferred long-term employee George Stooksbury for the Clerk's office, but that went as something of a perk or reward to longtime (37 years) commissioner Billy Tindell. The selection of Tindell made him ineligible to vote as a commissioner, even under the dubious rules we selected that kept the term-limited voting on their successors.

Presumably the "big plum" district that day was the fourth. Both of its seats would need appointments. So the commission chose to start there. Any commissioner could nominate someone or pass; audience members also could nominate someone. Then after the nominations, the voting would occur without speeches. The procedure was that the first candidate to secure a majority, ten votes, would be the appointment. After each round of voting, the candidate with the lowest vote total would be dropped, and rounds of voting would continue until an appointment.

That day I followed a pattern of nominating and sticking with the candidate of my choice until that candidate was eliminated. Then I'd go to my highest-rated choice left in the field. In the clash in the Fourth District, my choice was Elaine Davis, but the first seat in the Fourth District went to developer Richard Cate. For the second seat in that district the options narrowed down to a less-than-appealing choice between developer Scott Davis and sheriff-envoy Lee Tramel. I opted for Scott Davis only because of his public vow only to serve the interim period until the election. The 9-9 deadlock (Tindell was the 19th commissioner but now as the clerk-designate was ineligible to vote) set off waves of re-votes and recesses. I thought of passing because I did not like the choices, but could not in good conscience switch from one candidate to the other.

During one of those breaks I tried to look over heads and around elbows to the mess that was going on in the small corridor that linked the Large Assembly Room to a hallway and the Small Assembly Room. I later learned from news reports about an effort to get Cate sworn in early to break the deadlock on the other seat. Commissioner John Schmid caught wind of the ploy and confronted the new appointee; Cate backed down and decided to wait to the scheduled 2 p.m. swearing in of the new appointees. Meanwhile, the sheriff faction's Lee Tramel and Lumpy confronted Schmid. Tramel berated Schmid for missing a lot of meetings. Lumpy called the bald Schmid a peckerhead.[21]

The Third District's Tony Norman, like me elected less than six months earlier, found it surreal. "I was completely dumbfounded at what was taking place. And than I heard whispers in the back of someone being sworn in. What? What's going on?"[22]

At one point I found myself staring across the nearly empty dais to Seventh District Commissioner R. Larry Smith. He prided himself on interviewing all the roughly 70 candidates who had expressed an interest, but (we later learned) was upset that the Ninth District's Paul Pinkston and Larry Clark had settled on a process where a seven-person district committee they had appointed would come up with a name. The name was given to Pinkston and Clark in the deli area of the South Knoxville Bi-Lo. It turned out to be a little-known florist, Tim Greene. Smith nevertheless followed the pattern of deferring to the home district commissioners.[23]

Fourth District Commissioner Phil Guthe, one of the five who sued to void the charter, later published a book critical of term limits, and arguing for deference to the choice of the outgoing term-limits-avoiding commissioner in presumably all cases, not just the five of eight where it occurred.[24] Commissioner Paul Pinkston had argued for some, perhaps greater consideration to the opinions of those not term limited, those who would still be commissioners at the next meeting and would have to work with the appointee. His was a minority view.[25]

The use of the term "my district" is casual and frequent, but shouldn't be used in a possessive sense. It wasn't Phil Guthe's seat; it was a Fourth District seat and wasn't necessarily his to reward, no matter how much pique he expressed at that observation. Each elected and legally serving commissioner had been entrusted by our constituents with one vote, a vote of equal value to all other votes on the body. Some have skills of community connections, some have skills in research, some are skilled in the procedures and history of the legislative body, all have intriguing life experiences, and all must blend those skills to make informed choices through discussion not silent deference.

The deadlocked Fourth District seat was moved to the end of the agenda while we considered the other seats. I had asked First District Commissioner Diane Jordan to support Amy Broyles in the Second District. She leaned back in her chair and said that "those Orange Ballot people" had said some unkind things about her (she was one of those who sued to void the charter), so no she would not vote for Amy. She just before the vote asked me if I would nominate her son Josh for the First District. I leaned back in my chair and said no. She appeared startled.

*Commissioner Diane Jordan,
Clerk Designee Billy Tindell, and me.*

Photo by Jon Gustin.

So Diane Jordan nominated Josh Jordan. "Jordan nominates Jordan," stated the clerk to a few snicker and mutters in the audience. The commission majority followed her lead, fulfilling what Commissioner Tank Strickland earlier had said to me, "She'll keep the paycheck in the family." Commissioners later would learn that Josh Jordan once had been a crack dealer for a convicted killer.[26] (I should hasten to add that I sat next to Josh for several months on commission and he was a responsible and pleasant young man putting his life together).

The vote then moved to the Second District. Previously Billy Tindell had announced via faxes that Jonathan Wimmer was his choice, and some already were congratulating Wimmer on his presumptive selection by the larger body. I saw no need to overlook someone who had twice as many votes as Wimmer in both the primary and the forum. Behind me I could hear something of a "Wimmer, Wimmer" grunt/chant that might have been coming from Billy. "I nominate the people's choice in the Second District, Amy Broyles," I said. Then I heard Commissioner Tony Norman say Wimmer and shortly thereafter there was a commotion. Billy Tindell was at the floor microphone. Apparently my words had hit a chord, and Tindell was there to remind people who his choice was; Billy's "mah choice" apparently was more important than the people's choice.

I interrupted with a point of order that the commission had opted for no speeches, and this was not a nomination from the floor but a speech in favor of a name in nomination. The chair had to agree, and Tindell reluctantly left the floor microphone. No one person secured a majority on the first vote. Jonathan Wimmer rightly has been praised for not joining in an agreement to be selected, sworn in early, and cast a vote to tie-breaking vote for Tramel.[27] Amy and I also opposed such shenanigans. Our district's reward for the noble behavior of not dealing to swing another district was the Bolus ascendance—which succeeded after likely arm-twisting and the selective swearing-in plan. It should be noted that my first choice, Amy Broyles, was still on the table when the pressured switches to Bolus began. Even if I'd abandoned past practice and cast a vote for Wimmer (and somehow Schmid's vote followed me) that would not have gotten him to ten; and by then both those choices were verboten because they didn't advance the apparent "you're in, but you must be sworn in early and break the tie in our favor" plan.

Reporter Hubert Smith, left, looks on as competing Fourth District nominees Scott Davis and Lee Tramel talk with Commissioner Craig Leuthold, right.

Photo by Jon Gustin.

Commission proceeded through less tangled votes for the other appointments. As we came around once again to the deadlocked Fourth District seat, I notice Bolus seated across the room in the seat previously occupied by Billy Tindell. I expressed my surprise to the chairman and asked him to introduce the new person joining us. "This swearing-in really stinks up a process that already has started to smell," I said. Schmid added, "This is a legal move, but the intent of the move is to put in one candidate. It stinks to high heaven. It is an insult to Mr. Guthe [presumably by ignoring his preferred appointee]. It is an insult to the people of the 4th District." Commissioner Phil Guthe added, "I've been insulted before, and I'll be insulted again."[28] One also could add it was an affront to clear indications of public preference in the Second District. Around this time Becky was in the audience holding aloft a sign that read "This Really Stinks." The photo appeared the next day on the front of the *News Sentinel*.

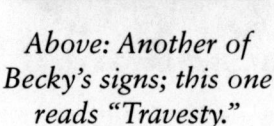

Above: Another of Becky's signs; this one reads "Travesty."

Upper right: Commissioners Mills and Clark.

Lower right: Charles Bolus sudden appearance at a chair on the dais.

Photos by Jon Gustin.

Nominee Scott Davis saw Bolus in a position to vote and recognized what was happening. Davis withdrew, and Tramel won the appointment with twelve votes. During one late break I met Bolus for the first time and was underwhelmed.

The meeting drew to its ignominious close. I mulled about and spoke to a few folks in the audience, all mutually stunned. Just before leaving, the now-former Sixth District Commissioner Mark Cawood approached me somberly and said, "You are an honorable man." He left to a job as a bailiff.

Reactions to the meeting were swift and appropriately negative. *News Sentinel* columnist Greg Johnson wrote:

> They left behind the detritus of democracy, the refuse of representative government, the offal of openness and a pile of political poo. Their actions when selecting replacements for the 12 term-limited officials ousted by the Supreme Court ruling were imperious, obnoxious and offensive. They used the term-limit turmoil to protect their progeny, honor their elders, suck up to their spouse and generally just smooch each other's derrieres....
>
> The landslides expose the backroom dealing that took place beforehand. The collusion continued during Wednesday's meeting when commissioners recessed so they could talk outside of the eyeshot and earshot of the public. That same collusion led to ousted commissioner Billy Tindell being appointed county clerk and ex-sheriff Tim Hutchison conveniently landing a $99,000 a year job as deputy to new Sheriff J. J. Jones. Through it all, commission chairman Moore's handling of the crisis was beyond bad. It was repugnant.... The measure of a man is taken in crisis and this crisis proved Moore arrogant, inept and disdainful of the voice of the people. The incestuous deal-making he brokered between small-minded politicians with a small-town mindset spoiled public trust and left a mess.[29]

Above: Reporters at the Black Wednesday appointments meeting.

Left: New commissioner Josh Jordan and former commissioner Diane Jordan.

Photos by Jon Gustin.

Becky and I went to lunch at the Copper Cellar restaurant to review the outrageous contrivance that was the appointments meeting. Fairly quickly the term Black Wednesday became the near-universal term for the fiasco.

Later an out-of-town reporter would offer the most succinct summary of the event. "At curtain's close," wrote Dan Barry, "the 12 appointments included the son of one outgoing commissioner, the wife of another outgoing commissioner, the father of a sitting commissioner, a top aide to the politically muscular sheriff, and a businessman who years earlier had come out on the wrong end of sexual harassment suit. It seems a catfish could have been appointed if properly connected."[30]

That evening and for several days the various local news web sites were alive with hundreds of posts on the commission's actions, expressed in several threads, almost always the posts were properly derisive of Black Wednesday but informed and polite. Some offered kind words to me regarding Monday's forum and Wednesday's county commission meeting. I wrote back, thanking all of those persons for being active citizens and demanding better government, one that is accountable and responsible, as well as open and honest.

"We all may come up short on some occasions, but it is nice to be recognized for trying to move in the proper direction," I wrote. "The past few days have seen many more disturbing revelations about some of the commission's choices and practices. I hope we can keep the conversations focused not on personal attacks on the people, but the repugnant procedures and poor policy choices made. I encourage people to contact the County Commission office (comission@knoxcounty.org or 865-215-2534) to sign up for the public comments section, and to show up at the next meeting (Feb. 26th, 2pm). Find and support good candidates. Point out when commission violates the spirit and possibly the letter of any law or our newly approved ethics code."

The evening of January 31, 2007, still reeling from that morning's shameful appointments meeting, I read online that my friend Molly Ivins had died late that afternoon. Molly was 62. She succumbed to a seven-year battle with breast cancer quietly at home surrounded by family and friends. Molly had an innate ability to find the absurdity in our politics; lambaste the mean, corrupt, and stupid; and still tell a great story and maintain a hearty laugh.[31] I leaned back in my chair and welled up a bit. She was so needed now, and she was gone.

6:
Trial and Tribulation

Herb Moncier is an unmade bed of a man. When he puts on a rumpled suit and points his scuffed wingtips toward a courtroom, however, he becomes a tenacious advocate. Herb can raise a pudgy finger skyward and demand justice rain down. He can offend the sensibilities of opponents and some judges, but he is tireless in pursuit of remedies to what he argues are Knox County's (especially the Sheriff's Office) legal offenses. It may be too much if every lawyer were like Herb, but I pity the poor community that doesn't have at least one Herb.

Naturally Herb and citizens outraged by Black Wednesday found each other. Their lawsuit, however, would be combined with one filed by *News Sentinel* editor Jack McElroy. McElroy's attorney was Rick Hollow, an expert who helped draft Tennessee's Open Meetings Law. Herb and the citizens held out for a jury trial. They got it. Knox County's Law Director, John Owings, and his staff would try to defend the commission's actions. Chancellor Daryl Fansler would hear the case. The players thus were set.

Technically Jack McElroy was suing in his capacity as an individual citizen, but that in no way should minimize the fact that local news media finally had awakened to the long-simmering abuses in Knox County government. Political scientist John Zaller has a term for it, the burglar alarm model. Modern U.S. news organizations rarely do much routine coverage of local governance, only rousing citizens from their slumber when something very wrong is in progress.[32]

During the Sunshine Trial all three local TV news operations had live shots from outside the courtroom, often featuring interviews with guest local lawyers. Newspaper coverage was extensive, and the local blogs were alive with updates and commentary. Even the few local outlets for radio news had some coverage.

Reporters crowd lawyers Moncier and Hollow, WATE anchor Gene Patterson set to interview Commissioner Scott Moore, WBIR Anchor Robin Wilhoit readies to talk to lawyer Don Bosch, a mobile courthouse hallway news operation.

Photos by Jon Gustin.

The trial, of course, was preceded by depositions. I gave a long and elaborate one, recalling with as much precision as possible all that had happened before and during the meeting. I had been on the short end of too many 18-1 and 17-2 votes on the procedural matters leading up to Black Wednesday. So I had no illusions the law director perspective on these matters would be in any way close to mine, or matching my interests. So, I brought along my friend Jim Andrews as an attorney. I'd managed Jim's nearly successful campaign for sheriff, and I knew he'd give good advice as needed. Jim also accompanied me to the morning of the testimony, most likely an enraging sight to the commission contingent devoted to Sheriff Tim Hutchison.

Herb had indicated he only needed me to verify some faxes. I'd be done in twenty minutes. That proved to be quite an underestimate. For three and a half hours I testified, covering everything from routine meeting operation, to the factions on commission, to my forum reviewing the candidates, to my contacts with other commissioners in the days leading up to Black Wednesday.

The Law Director had crafted a narrow definition of "deliberation" that he believed led to a generous definition of what contact commissioners could have with each other and still be in compliance with the Open Meetings Act.

My guess is that both Moncier and Hollow saw an opportunity to question a witness who was willing to speak in great detail about his contacts and what was happening. I spoke about how the Black Wednesday meeting came to be, and how commission curiously allowed persons determined ineligible to serve nevertheless would be voting on their replacements. These I called "zen" positions. The occupants were not there for the purpose of a vacancy, but there for the purpose of voting.

Several competing ignoble instincts were at work: the battle between competing mayor and sheriff factions, the treatment of commission districts as little fiefdoms for favors to be doled out to family and friends, and the insistence of deference to the departing commissioners' wishes—despite their contrivance to remain on the ballot, and their dubious case for eligibility to vote on successors. These ignoble instincts crashed into each other on Black Wednesday in full view of a disbelieving public.

I laid it all out—the good, bad, ugly, sad, ironic, and silly. The first moments were uneventful, merely verifying some faxes, but then Moncier and Hollow began to plumb the items in my exhaustive deposition and then lay them before the jury. I described my view of the factions on commission, the pre-meeting maneuvers, the lobbying and phone calls, and the operation of Black Wednesday itself. "But what Harmon ultimately did on the witness stand Wednesday was to lay bare the politics of government that the public rarely sees or hears about," wrote Jamie Satterfield for the *News Sentinel*.[33]

Two rows of commissioners watching the Sunshine Trial.

Photo by Jon Gustin.

Left:
News Sentinel
Editor Jack
McElroy,

Right:
Chancellor
Daryl Fansler.

Photos by
Jon Gustin.

I spoke about a conversation I had with Commissioner Thomas "Tank" Strickland about what his seatmate, Diane Jordan would do regarding her replacement. He told me she'd nominate her husband or son. "She'll keep the paycheck in the family," he said. I admitted to an understanding I had with Lumpy that I'd back his choice in the 5th district if he'd back my choice in the 2nd. The deal fell apart well before the meeting, and I regret even trying it. I spoke about the "gentlemen's agreement" in which a lot of commissioners unquestioningly would back the replacement choice of the departing commissioner. Of course, I also spoke about the chaotic recesses and manipulations in the 4th district tie vote. That, of course, was connected to the Bolus early swearing in. I repeated the previously noted conversation when Lumpy phoned me as Becky and I were on our way to the meeting. "It's going to be Bolus," he said.[34]

Foreground: Herb Moncier.
Background: John Owings and Mary Ann Stackhouse

Photo by Jon Gustin.

I couldn't tell for certain, but it appeared to me that Law Director John Owings was spending a lot of time on a cell phone during my testimony. Behind him in the audience gallery of the courtroom stoically sat a group of commissioners. Clearly many were unhappy and would try to vilify me for what happened; I had broken the unspoken rule of silence about the misdeeds.

Deputy Law Director Mary Ann Stackhouse spent the better part of an hour trying to poke holes in my testimony. It didn't have much effect, especially when she spun such farfetched concoctions such as I was trying to reduce the number of voters so I'd have more power—as if losing votes 10-1 was of such greater value than losing them 18 to 1. At one point in the banter I joked, "I thought you were my lawyer."[35] The whole surreal experience came to an end and I went home. Becky saw the large photo of me the next day in the paper, immediately noticing I needed a haircut and should have worn a different shirt.

The hours after my testimony yielded some astounding reactions. Jamie Satterfield of the *News Sentinel* ran a thorough and fair news account to which an editor had affixed a strange headline "Harmon accused of political agenda" in the print edition, but howls of protest led online to the better "Harmon becomes star witness for sunshine plaintiffs, exposes secrecy." The subhead was "County law official tries to discredit commissioner's testimony." It seems odd in the print headline to reach down to the minor detail of Stackhouse's effort to reframe the testimony, odder still to accuse a politician of being political. Perhaps it says something about the state of disgust for politics or the state of our language that terms for elections, public policy, and self-governance are disdainful by connotation.

The day after the testimony Amy Broyles had arranged an activity at the old courthouse. Dozens of her supporters would show up to sign her ballot petition. Moments after she picked it up, she'd be able to return it with more than the required number of signatures. When Becky and I joined that line, the others spontaneously applauded.

Hiker and TVUUC minister Chris Buice during that time sat down on a bench near an old man wearing a sour expression. They talked and the subject of county commission came up. Chris mentioned that one member of his congregation, Mark Harmon, was on commission. "I know him," said the old man.

"Uh-oh," thought Chris, "here it comes."

"They should build a statue of him," the old man said.

One enthusiastic blogger came to my defense online, even comparing me to civil rights hero and Supreme Court Justice Thurgood Marshall. The praises were way over the top, but made me feel better during a time when clash and anger were at a high pitch.

The trial was well covered in the *New Sentinel*, but that coverage was not the only evidence the "burglar alarm" was ringing in local newsrooms. The *News Sentinel* in the aftermath of Black Wednesday ran an article explaining, "At least 13 of 19 commissioners either work for Knox County or have relatives who do, drawing nearly $900,000 per year in taxpayer-funded salaries." The article even had an elaborate graphic linking commissioners (shown in photos) to their county jobs and the county jobs held by relations.[36] After the September 1, 2010, swearing-in of the new commission, *News Sentinel* editor Jack McElroy delighted in the revolution in county government that enforced term limits and brought in fresh faces. He noted that only one of the commissioners, city police officer Brad Anders, worked any other local government job.[37]

Eventually Knox County Commission had to do the appointments all over, this time using a public process. That meeting proceeded smoothly, at times we startled ourselves at how civil, cooperative, and non-partisan we were. At one point, imploring my colleagues not to shoot down a candidate merely because she'd run as a Democrat, I said, "I've voted for more Republicans [today] than I ever have in my life."[38]

Not all the developments in the aftermath of Black Wednesday, however, were uplifting. Proof that "no good deed goes unpunished" the citizen plaintiffs in the sunshine lawsuit suddenly found themselves in an odd spot. After the jury's guilty verdict, somehow the cases were "unmerged." The citizen case was dismissed, and the citizens assessed costs. Bills delineating various costs were sent not to the lawyer, the usual procedure, but to the homes of those citizen plaintiffs. The group reformed to create a Charter Defense Fund, raising money to settle the more than $33,000 in court costs. It should be noted that none of that money went to Herb Moncier; he took the case effectively pro bono, contingent on fees being levied against the defendants, something that did not happen. I contributed some of my discretionary money to that defense fund—because such public service should be honored not levied fees.[39]

Three of the citizen plaintiffs in the Sunshine Lawsuit: Jerry Bone, Bee DeSelm and Jim Gray (left to right).

Photo by Jon Gustin.

7:
It Just Buffoons Me

Very early on settlers in the Southern Colonies began to venture out of their cities and towns and began to engage in extensive farming and ranching enterprises. Hence, the need for broad regional governments arose much sooner than in the north, before cities and towns could become well established as a political force. Additionally, many of the wealthy and powerful citizens owned large plantations and lived far from cities and towns, lending political muscle to the impetus for counties. Early on counties were established and given broad judicial and legislative powers. Instead of the county board and officers being ex-officio, they mostly elected, giving southern counties independence from city and town governments.

—Danny S. Batts II,
"Attitudes and Perceptions of County Legislators Regarding Their Influence Over the Formulation and Implementation of Environmental Policy," Masters of Public Administration Thesis, Texas State University, Spring 2005.[40]

One maddening distinction kept coming up during Knox County Commission's meetings, county versus city. Some persons lived inside the city limits of Knoxville; some lived outside those limits. Those inside the limits paid additional taxes for additional services, but all counted on Knox County for schools and libraries. All paid Knox County taxes and all deserved a county commission responsive to their needs.

Foremost at needlessly cleaving city versus county distinctions was Scott "Scoobie" Moore. During one review of some county program, he asked what portion of the participants were from the county. A frustrated Commissioner Sam McKenzie asked, "Wouldn't that, by definition, be all of them?"

Left:
Commissioner Scott "Scoobie" Moore.

Below:
Commissioner Greg "Lumpy" Lambert gives a TV interview.

Photos by Jon Gustin.

Scoobie and friends also presented a journalistic quandary. Are reporters obliged to clean up politicians' grammar? Scoobie tended to pronounce libraries like lie-berries, and indigent something like IN-jih-dint. One reporter, following a particularly egregious meeting, presented an eye/ear witness account of what actually was said.

Scoobie-isms that day included "as soon as something has came out," and "They's been a lot of people." On permitting the ethics committee to make recommendations to commission, he blurted that the committee was appointed to do "a pacific job." His most-quoted line by political wags also came during a discussion in which he wished to limit the role of the ethics committee. "This buffoons me, this just buffoons me," he said.

Lumpy took exception to the ethics committee being allowed to make recommendations on nepotism and other conflicts. "This is reminiscent of the Inquisition, the Salem Witch Trials, the McCartney hearings," said the Lumpster.

"I don't agree with the comparison to the Inquisition, the Salem Witch Trials and I hope Mr. Lambert meant the McCarthy Hearings. I am not familiar with the McCartney hearings," I replied. Reporter Betty Bean asked, "Weren't the McCartney hearings held when Yoko Ono broke up the Beatles?"[41]

The sunshine lawsuit verdict left the commission once again with just eleven members. We once again had eight colleagues to select, plus four more interim offices for fee offices. The penalty for violating the state's open meetings act was that the actions previously done were null and void. Chancellor Fansler also added that any future violation of the act would be contempt of his court order. We also had specific instructions that read a lot like a consent settlement I had suggested and my colleagues had rejected. Only the remaining eleven would vote. We would hold a public process and a public meeting.

You might think that such a judicial rebuke might leave us more polite and circumspect, and that by mere reduced numbers of commissioners our meetings would be shorter. Uh, no, not even close. The remaining commissioners sometimes would go out of their way to weave bizarre scenarios and odd extrapolations trying to cast the sunshine law itself as unworkable. It was a strange Alphonse and Gaston routine that grew stale long before it stopped being repeated. Some meetings stretched to nine or ten hours. Becky stopped baking and sending cookies for the group in protest. Our reputation as a dysfunctional body had extended so far that the *New York Times* sent a reporter.

The reporter noted how commission chair Scott Moore and Mayor Mike Ragsdale bantered in mutual contempt. One commissioner complained about what the reporter called "sheriff's department lackeys cackling in the back of the room, prompting a nearly physical confrontation at recess." The most remembered item, however, of that seven-hour meeting probably was this Lumpy moment:

> ...he leveled his blunderbuss at another commissioner, a university professor named Mark Harmon, who had done nothing more to antagonize than open the meeting with a reflection that referred to 'the inherent dignity of every person.'
>
> Thus Lumpy spoke. In defending why county employees should be allowed to hold county office, he rambled about poor people in need of jobs, then channeled their imagined thoughts about Mr. Harmon, the academic: 'And what they say is, 'How does that arrogant little university twit sit up there and make those decisions that keep us from having jobs?'
>
> Shouts, calls for order, calls for an apology that never came....[42]

Fortunately, Becky came up with an appropriate reply, T-shirts distributed at cost at the next meeting.

I dismissed the whole thing as just Lumpy being Lumpy. I was more concerned with the false assertion that I couldn't understand working class concerns. My family grew up "not poor, just broke," and concern for the working class is deeply woven into my personal being and political philosophy.

The incident became a term and touchstone for my time on county commission, and the subtitle for this book. If you "google" the phrase University Twit, the first thing that appears is a picture of me in the T-shirt. When Becky told my sister Pam to try this online search, I heard the laughter coming through the phone line and across the room.

8:
Spiritual Home

I call that mind free, which sets no bounds to its love, which is not imprisoned in itself or in a sect, which recognizes in all human beings the image of God and the rights of his children, which delights in virtue and sympathizes with suffering wherever they are seen, which conquers pride, anger, and sloth, and offers itself up a willing victim to the cause of mankind.
—William Ellery Channing,
Spiritual Freedom, 1830

I was raised Catholic. In fact, during elementary school years my mother briefly tried to put my sister and me in parochial school. That experiment barely lasted a month. My sister was being beaten over handwriting technique by a senile, 90-year-old lay instructor. I was in trouble in math class for getting the right answer the wrong way.

So we lived near St. Bernard's Catholic Church and School, but walked several blocks to Kelton Elementary. Owing to various saint holidays, early June found us in summer break while the St. Bernard's kids still walked past our house on the way to school. Budding entrepreneurs that we were, the Harmon kids grabbed the opportunity.

We plugged in the Vac-U-Form, a toy that allowed us to bake the accompanying colors of goo into plastic spiders and worms. Other kids may have settled for a pedestrian lemonade stand. We bellowed and beckoned, "Bugs for Sale!" It wasn't long before multicolored worms and spiders were popping up on various St. Bernard's desks and tables. It didn't take the nuns long to discuss the source of the offense, call our mother, and shut down our budding business.

Shortly thereafter the local parochial schools raised tuition, effectively forcing large numbers of poor students out of Catholic education and into public schools. Parents, of course, still sent those kids to Sunday morning CCD (religious education) classes. Often those consisted of bored teenagers asking, "What was today's Gospel about?" Equally bored students made up generic responses or interpretations. This pattern did not create a problem until First Holy Communion neared, and the nuns belatedly realized the Catholic School kids knew the lyrics to be sung, but not the CCD kids. We were told to follow the melody and quietly sing "loo-loo-loo." So, of course, parents were treated on that solemn occasion to a loud chorus of improvised "LOO-LOO-LOOs," drowning out any lyrics remembered by our snickering Catholic School cohorts.

As my brother, sister, and I grew, our direct contacts with the church largely were limited to Sundays. Sometimes I'd shoot hoops in the church parking lot. The old cemetery across the street from the church also bordered our back yard. So we'd scamper over an old stump and fallen fence to play ball games in the summer and ride sleds in the winter.

It's certainly possible my Irish Catholic background played a role when I interviewed at Xavier University in Cincinnati for my first teaching job. The selection committee, including Ms. Boyle, Father Flynn, and Father Hagerty, certainly gave the young Syracuse University graduate, Harmon, a chance.

Religious expression also played a surprising role in my doctoral work. Mine may well be the first documented case of prayer assisting a dissertation. My self-selected project, needed to complete my PhD program at Ohio University, was a massive content analysis of news selection patterns in local television newscasts. The file grew to be so large it would not run under the standard faculty space allowance on the mid-1980s university mainframe computer. So I went to mass at Xavier's chapel several weeks in a row, sitting in front so Father Ferguson would see me. He not only served mass, but also was the computer services director. Thus properly prefaced, he approved my request for added computer space. The project ran. The defense was successful; and my doctoral program was complete.

I started attending Unitarian Universalist services when I lived in Lubbock, Texas. I'd moved there to teach at Texas Tech. Several friends attended the "UU" church, and Minister Tom Perchlik spoke to themes I found important and compelling.

When I moved to Knoxville, I tried out the Tennessee Valley Unitarian Universalist Church (TVUUC). It was a large congregation, but Wade Till, former Democratic Party chair, was pleased to meet me and to speak with a former Democratic candidate and county chair. Two or three times I checked out the smaller Westside Unitarian Universalist congregation. Both were nice, but eventually I drifted into regular attendance at TVUUC.

In fact, it was at TVUUC that I met Becky. She invited me to lunch about two seconds before I was to ask her the same. Two hours passed in an instant as we conversed easily and happily. We began dating and then TVUUC played a more pivotal role in our lives—as the site of our wedding, June 14, 2003.

The wedding was a delight for all who attended. Even one cranky wedding scrooge had to admit he enjoyed it. The ceremony was brief and personally meaningful. Becky and I selected the reading and vows. TVUUC's minister, Chris Buice, remembered a church fundraiser during which Becky dressed as a clown and I wore a frog costume. "Some faiths may frown upon mixed marriages, but we Unitarian Universalists take a different view," he said. "Joy and best wishes to clown and frog."

Becky glowed with beauty. Her sister Judy was the maid of honor. My niece Kelley was so happy to be our flower girl. I'd planned on my brother Michael as best man, but his untimely death months earlier put my nephew Mack beside me as best man.

June 14, 2003: Becky, Mark, and best man Mack

The wedding was in the TVUUC sanctuary and the reception followed immediately just a hallway away in the church fellowship hall. The klezmer band, Tennessee Schmaltz, may have taken by surprise some of Becky's Baptist work colleagues from UT Medical Center. My university colleagues and Democratic Party friends quickly got into the spirit. Music, food, and drink flowed merrily. Nine-year-old Mack stood up to give a toast. "To Mark and Becky," he said (long pause, the planned words bride and groom were not forthcoming), "the wedding people." "The wedding people!" toasted the giddy crowd. Five-year-old Kelley literally was hopping up and down with glee, so much so it was difficult to keep the bow in the back of her dress from falling apart.

So it was that TVUUC became our spiritual home. Chris Buice was such an eloquent and thoughtful pastor. He could weave together traditional scripture, jokes, and stories to suit topics as broad as the value of doubt, the poetry of Rumi, the lyrics of the Beatles, or the spirituality of Star Trek.

I served a term on the church board. I even wrote a lay service based on my interest in radio. The "readings" were from Edward R. Murrow speeches and commentaries. In place of the homily was my radio play, *Jesus and Buddha on Talk Radio*. Later I wrote a ditty about my early experiences on county commission. *Knox County Commission: The Play*, combined with an accompanying pork dinner, became a heavily bid item at a church auction.

Becky became very active in the church rummage sale. The rummage sale was huge. It occupied the bulk of the building and spilled outside. The days of sorting and pricing incoming items left me as support staff, bringing food to Becky and her cadre of volunteers. Often I'd be called upon to set up or break down tables, working with Greg McKendry, a burly bear of a man with an easy smile and stories to share.

In late July of 2008 Greg's wife Barbara was creating costumes for a summer children's musical workshop at the church. Becky, who has experience in theatrical staging, had been helping behind the scenes as well. The kids were doing a condensed version of *Annie* called *Annie Jr*. Becky reported the rehearsals had gone really well, and we set out that Sunday morning to the special performance.

July 27, 2008, dawned warm and bright. Jim David Adkisson, an unemployed truck driver filled with rage, left his home in Powell, Tennessee. He drove past several other churches conducting services; he knew where he was going, and what he planned to do. His residence did not hold many books, mostly the diatribe-filled screeds from the hate hustlers of talk radio and TV: *Liberalism is a Mental Disorder* by Michael Savage; *Let Freedom Ring: Winning the War of Liberty over Liberalism* by Sean Hannity; *The O'Reilly Factor: The Good, The Bad, and the Completely Ridiculous in American Life* by Bill O'Reilly.

Adkisson tragically had bought the crap that liberals and Democrats were the source of his problems. He mixed in a strong doses of the homophobia also prevalent in hate radio. Adkisson knew of TVUUC because one of his former wives, one of many failed relationships, had taken him there a couple times in the 1990s. He scribbled a note that because he could not get to liberals and Democrats at the national level, he'd kill those who voted for them. He added to that some homophobic rants. He quoted Bernard Goldberg's *The 100 People Who Are Screwing Up America*. He put the note in the car along with the shotgun he had modified to fit in the guitar case. He also had a bag with 76 shells of #4 shot. He envisioned a massacre and eventual police standoff from which he would not return.

Becky was running errands for the play's operation, so I entered the sanctuary and sat alone on one side. My friend Amy Broyles, her husband Jamie Parkey, and their two daughters, Aidyn and Avery, were already there on the opposite side of the sanctuary. Little Avery toddled across to grab my hand and lead me to sit with them.

Jamie's daughter Amira had the coveted role of Miss Hannigan. The only adult in the cast was my friend and fellow professor John Bohstedt, chrome-domed, dressed as Daddy Warbucks, and awaiting his entrance from the same hallway where Becky was working. Avery had grown fussy during the first musical number, so Amy sat with her in the glass-enclosed cry room.

Amira had just begun her lines when Adkisson walked into the church and the hallway leading to the sanctuary. He reached the sanctuary entrance, removed his gun from the guitar case, and pointed it toward the pews, stage left of the altar. Usher Greg McKendry was near Adkisson. Greg's broad body took the bulk of the first blast.

Like most of the audience I was focused on the play. For me the first jarring moment was aural, the ear-splitting bang. Instinctively I turned and headed under the pew as the second blast rang out. On the way down I caught a glimpse of Adkisson, curly gray hair, silver barrel of a gun in hand, eyes fixed and expressionless—a portrait in the ferocious banality of evil.

I peeked at the pew behind me where a woman, clearly in shock, gently was touching the many spots on her torso from which she was bleeding.

Becky ran to the office and likely was the first of many 911 calls. John Bohstedt rushed the gunman and tackled him. Jamie Parkey had pushed his daughter Aidyn under the pew and also jumped on the gunman. Two other church members, Robert Birdwell and Terry Uselton, also got there quickly to restrain the gunman. Some other church members joined in holding Adkisson down. They wrestled away his gun and pinned his arms. Reportedly he said something like, "Hey, you're hurting me" as the carnage he had wrought played out.

Greg bled to death on the cold floor of the church he loved. Linda Kraeger, a visitor from Westside, part of a family there to see *Annie Junior,* lay dying. Six others were seriously injured, some severely.

There were so many heroes during those frantic minutes. Greg no doubt saved many lives, including my own. The brave men who rushed toward and tackled the gunman saved many lives. Ann Snyder had blocked Adkisson during his guitar-case-toting arrival, from the rear doors and sent him to the front. That effectively prevented him from shooting in the same area as the child performers. Music Director Vicki Masters' shouts got all of us quickly moving to exits. Religious Education Director Brian Griffin hurried the children from their classrooms up the hill to Second Presbyterian Church.

Many of us found ourselves on a slope outside the church, shocked but sharing information as best we could. Word had come that Brian had gotten the children to safety, but that Greg likely wouldn't make it. Police and ambulance units began coming and going. I suggested in a loud voice that we should pray in whatever way each wanted, and that we use our cell phones to call a well-positioned relative as a central point of contact for what was happening. Word soon would reach our startled friends, neighbors, and relatives. I learned

Amy had been crouched on the floor of the cry room, shielding her daughter Avery, only feet and a doorway away from the gunman. Aidyn's distress at first was about how her new dress had blood stains.

I found Becky and held her tightly. By this point policemen were asking us to wait in various rooms where we would be explained next steps in the investigation and prosecution. On the last moments of cell phone power I got word to my sister that Becky and I were okay.

After a couple hours we were able to go home. Becky and I handled a lot of news inquiries. It seemed both necessary and inevitable, given my roles as both journalism professor and public official. We monitored television, radio, and web coverage, and also gave both phone and in-person interviews. In all we tried to stress the resilience, courage, and grace of the people with whom we worshipped. One interview of us by the local NBC affiliate, WBIR, found its way via satellite onto the *Today* show and several newscasts around the globe.

The following Monday was a county commission meeting. I told my colleagues, that I had to leave the meeting early for a special service to be held that evening at Second Presbyterian. The skies had opened and a driving rain was underway. I quoted the old blues lyric, "The Sky is Cryin." Becky and I huddled under an umbrella and eventually found space in the crowded pews.

The service that day was an incredible display of the entire Knoxville community's better angels. People from all walks of life and congregations were crammed side by side not merely in shared grief but in solidarity. One gunman had severed himself so much from people that he could not see his shared humanity with the people before him. Here friend and stranger alike shed tears of sorrow and joy, clasping hands and gazing intently eye to eye. When the hands went up for who was from other congregations, the huge number of visitor's hands drew applause from the UUs attending.

The actual vigil ceremony was simple, a few songs and messages. Reverend Chris Buice of TVUUC and Reverend Mitra Jafarzadeh of Westside had small roles, as did several other religious leaders, but the president of the Unitarian Universalist Association, Reverend William G. Sinkford, spoke to the greater themes at play, even ad-libbing a bit when a snap of thunder roared during one passage. Sinkford said that this shooting will not change who we are and what we believe; we may be feeling anger, but remember we also are filling with understanding and compassion. He also stated that the tragedy had forged a power in community that should not fade away. Unannounced on the program the service ended with the UU children from the play, led by the music director. They simply came to the center of the altar and started singing:

> *When you're faced with a day that's grey and lonely*
> *I just stick out my chin and grin and say*
> *The sun will come out tomorrow...*
> *Tomorrow... you're only a day away.*[43]

As the first few notes rang out, one almost could hear the crowd in unison saying, "Oh, no, it isn't. No, it can't be. Oh, it is. Yes, how perfect." They were belting out "Tomorrow" from *Annie*. The crowd joined in, swaying, hugging, and lighting vigil candles. Strangers held hands and shouted the chorus to the rafters. Roared approval. Hugs. Then Home. The sky was still crying.

The next several days the church was the center of a large and largely self-directed healing process. Flowers, cards, and messages came from across the globe. Food from around the area was available in the Fellowship Hall. Our greater UU church sent a crisis response team. Counselors were available at almost any hour. City firemen cleaned our sanctuary. John Gill from the District Attorney's office explained the prosecution process. Adkisson's hate remained. He later told police that he was depressed and unemployed, and chose to target our "ultraliberal" church because it "never met a pervert they just didn't embrace."[44] Later Adkisson would plead guilty and get the sentence that was the majority, and close to consensus, view of our congregation. He'd never walk freely again among civilized men and women.

Our church community managed to keep private from news coverage a ceremony to honor Greg and Linda. Then we held a very public rededication of our sanctuary to peace and love. Guitars, minus cases, were played during a musical interlude. Chris Buice spoke from the very spot of the shooting and reclaimed the space for all of us, for the inherent dignity and worth of all people, for our interconnected world, and for our shared humanity. One now could meet in the Greg McKendry Fellowship Hall, or check out books at the Linda Kraeger library in the room next to the pastor's office. We had back our spiritual home.

9:
Hate and the Church Shooting /
Standing on the Side of Love

In the aftermath of the shooting, of course, our lives individually and collectively were different. It would be impossible to return to any state of being before the blasts. We'd each have to incorporate the scar into the narratives of our lives, and somehow we did at varying paces and in different ways.

The congregation itself grew. Local people who learned of us first through the shootings came to console or check out, and some stayed. One aspect of the ordeal stuck with me, the role of hate speech. The killer likely had no idea that there before him were County Commissioner Mark Harmon, school board member Indya Kincannon and her children, and a county commission candidate, Amy Broyles, and her children. He could not know that I, for example, had published an article tearing apart Bernard Goldberg's erroneous conclusions, flawed claims, and bitter personalization of argument.[45] After all, Goldberg's blurt of a book was not about the 100 worst ideas, or the 100 worst policies, it was bashing 100 people.

I had an exchange of correspondence with an editor at National Public Radio, and scripted a commentary. This was the first draft:

> *That dark moment, eight days ago, I was seated in the very area the gunman was shooting toward. You likely have heard the stories of heroism and the global response of love and concern.*

But there is one more story to tell. In the frenzy following the shooting, some talk radio hosts became very defensive.

The accused shooter in his home had books from Bill O'Reilly, Sean Hannity, and Michael Savage.

"Don't blame those words," they bellowed. "That's as silly as blaming the car he drove." Well, no, but it was a rebuttal to an argument that never came.

I'm sure some did talk about guns, violence, or hate speech becoming hate action. Around here, however, the emphasis has been on love, unity, hope, and healing.

We really don't need to linger on cause and effect. The fact is hate speech can be criticized on ethical and moral grounds.

Yes, you are constitutionally protected in calling persons arrogant, godless, degenerates, and traitors. You can swipe at people instead of ideas or actions. You may even build an audience.

Our talk radio airwaves are filled with persons willing to spout off with personal attacks. I worry children will grow up thinking that is how you should argue. I worry they'll never hear respectful disagreement buttressed by supporting information. I'm concerned they'll not value genuine listening.

I'm a former college debater and a current county commissioner. I know the joy in winning an argument or an election. But winning can't be everything. The process we use to get there is our legacy to the next generation.

Much talk radio is a burnt-out shell of self-immolating hatred. I doubt it can be reformed, but hope it can be put off in the corner, a vile backwater whose practitioners are increasingly irrelevant and ignored.

The editor wrote back that she needed a bit more of narrative. "Most folks haven't heard this story," she wrote. Shudder. She wanted an intro about the basics of the news, and a "back announce" where I describe myself in one sentence. She also instructed "write YOUR story in a narrative—about 400 words."

So draft two was as follows:

ANNOUNCER: *The Tennessee Valley Unitarian Universalist Church today is back to more normal operation. Sunday the Knoxville church had a service to rededicate to peace the sanctuary where a gunman killed two people and injured six.*

Mark Harmon is a member of that church. He was there when the gunman shot. He also is an associate professor of journalism and electronic media at the University of Tennessee, and that leads him to one more story about the shooting and its aftermath.

COMMENTARY: *The dark moment when the shotgun blasts rang out I was seated in the general area the gunman was shooting. My wife was in the hallway, feet away from the first blast. The body of a friend, Greg McKendry, shielded many of us from harm. Other Unitarians tackled the gunman and saved many more lives. Greg and a visitor from another congregation, Linda Kraeger, were dead. Six more were hospitalized.*

You may have heard the stories of heroism and the global response of love and concern. Those are the major stories as we incorporate this outburst into the narrative of our lives.

But there is one story deserving less mention. Following the shooting, talk radio hosts became very defensive. The accused shooter had written of his hatred for liberals. He had in his home books, from Bill O'Reilly, Sean Hannity, and Michael Savage.

"Don't blame those words," they bellowed. "That's as silly as blaming the car he drove." Well, not quite, but it was an anticipatory reply to an argument that never came.

I'm sure someone did take the moment to talk about guns, or violence, or when hate speech becomes hate action. Around here, however, our emphasis has been on love, unity, hope, and healing.

Hateful diatribes likely played some role in the shooter's venom toward liberals and the targeting of my church. But that's a matter for the trial and for reflection from a distance of weeks or months.

Hate radio can and should be criticized on its own, on ethical and moral grounds. However, this is not their story—and it should not be contorted to their favorite subject, themselves.

It is our story, the people who were there watching a performance of the musical Annie Junior, *the culmination of a summer musical workshop for kids. Greg McKendry's widow, Barbara, worked for months on the costumes. It is the story of retired history professor John Bohstedt. John—in Daddy Warbucks costume—was the first to tackle the gunman. It is the story of Greg and Linda, their honorable and joyous lives cut short in an instant of hate-filled madness. It is the story of hundreds of congregations and thousands of individuals who have rushed to our aid for healing. Just as we have reclaimed our sanctuary as a house of peace and love, we hold close to our story—one of heroic and generous community.

TAG (BACK ANNOUNCE): Mark Harmon teaches journalism and broadcasting courses at the University of Tennessee. He also is a Knox County Commissioner and a proud member of the Tennessee Valley Unitarian Universalist Church.

The NPR editor wrote back that she still wanted more of my story, but that wasn't the shooting story I wanted to tell others then or now. I see the journalistic attraction of the more personal, less national story, one that fits a style of news story telling. But this very act of bucking certain frames only creates others. I was on the other side of the news, and it was quite a revelation to this journalist and journalism instructor.

Several months later I made another attempt to tell that broader story to a news audience. Though not picked up, it took the form of this note:

An Open Letter to Pastor Ken Pagano, New Bethel Church, Louisville, Kentucky
From: Mark Harmon, survivor of TVUUC shooting, Knoxville, Tennessee

Pastor Pagano, you have scheduled a church event in which you've encouraged the attending congregation to bring unloaded guns to your church. This event is scheduled eleven months to the day after a gunman came into my church and shot into the crowd watching the performance of a children's play.

A friend of mine died that day, "bleeding out" onto the cold floor of the church he loved. A visitor from a neighboring congregation died from her wounds. Several others were injured quite severely. I watched as one pew away a woman, clearly in shock, gently was touching the places from which her blood was squirting. Many of us physically unhurt are still recovering from this heinous act of hate.

In all their names I implore you, please stop your gun-toting grandstanding.

There is a reason the word sanctuary has a long association with churches. A church should be a place of unity, not division; hope, not fear; peace, not war;

justice, not vengeance. A church should be a place where a person can go to escape the worst of human behavior, and to find community with others humbly seeking to be better—whether one finds inspiration in that quest through God, the Bible, other texts, other names for God, or simply, as Abraham Lincoln put it, a recognition of the better angels of our nature.

The tranquility of a church is assured by reverence and respect, not mutual fear of an armed neighbor. Any suggestion the latter is needed is a vile insult to churchgoers. Greater carnage at our church was avoided not by retaliatory gunfire but by a handful of courageous men, some in their fifties and sixties, who rushed and tackled the gunman. The first to arrive was a 64-year-old history professor dressed for the day as Daddy Warbucks.

We know from harsh experience the toxic mess when hate and weapons mix with fragile, weak men who no longer see others as part of a shared humanity. It happened at the federal building in Oklahoma City. It happened at the 16th Street Baptist Church in Birmingham to four little girls. It happened at the Tennessee Valley Unitarian Universalist Church. It happened just recently to a doctor ushering at the Reformation Lutheran Church in Wichita, Kansas, to two soldiers standing outside a recruiting office in Arkansas, and to a security guard at the Holocaust Museum in Washington, D. C.

The numbers are clear. Each year our nation suffers a staggering toll of souls lost to gun-related suicides, accidents, and escalated arguments. Guns do not counter despair, fear, and hate. Guns only heighten the likelihood these emotional combinations will lead to tragedy. Legal culpability normally and properly rests only with the gunmen themselves, but just as we speak out about cultural failings in our mediated and personal environments, shouldn't we speak out against the repeated delusion that satisfaction can spew from the barrel of a gun?

You have, of course, every legal right to complete your planned and grotesque stunt. You can, and likely will, claim that recent court cases ignoring the militia clause make gun ownership as constitutionally protected as free speech. This letter is not a call to use the power of any state actor to stop you; it is an ethical plea to stop yourself, to reflect and to reason.

The hate-filled diatribes on talk radio will not stop. The personal-attack mongers on Fox News will prattle on unabated, but your change of heart would speak volumes to a world ready for reconciliation.

Dr. Mark D. Harmon is a member of the Tennessee Valley Unitarian Universalist Church. He is an associate professor of Journalism and Electronic Media at the University of Tennessee, Knoxville. He also is an elected county commissioner in Knox County, Tennessee.

At the start of 2011 several members of our congregation began to be more comfortable speaking about the shooting, prompted in some ways by a horrific shooting in Tucson, Arizona. The attack left a six dead including a federal judge and a nine year-old girl; thirteen were wounded, including Congresswoman Gabrielle Giffords.[46]

Within a few days of Tucson came word that a Knoxville gun shop and shooting range, Frontier Firearms, planned a charitable fundraiser during which participants could shoot at bobblehead dolls of Lane and Monte Kiffin, a head football coach and his father and assistant coach. Both abruptly left the University of Tennessee and also left some bad feelings among fans. The charity beneficiary, Second Harvest Food Bank, heard from several outraged persons. Director Elaine Streno stated, "The one organized movement from the Tennessee Valley Unitarian Universalist Church was kind and asked me to reconsider." She did and withdrew. The church raised a substantial amount of money for Second Harvest to replace any loss to that organization. The gun shop also changed course. The bobbleheads instead of being shot could be adopted by visitors.[47] At that Sunday's service TVUUC Minister Chris Buice relayed word of the outcome, praised our tradition of tolerance even for the most despised in a community, and plopped two bobbleheads down on the lectern where he was speaking.

Just a couple weeks later several interfaith groups conducted a "Standing on the Side of Love" event at our congregation, an event designed to start with the romantic love of Valentine's Day and take an even broader approach regarding the importance of love in combating hate. It was part of a larger national Unitarian Universalist Association movement with the same goal. First and foremost it was a positive response to the TVUUC shooting, but it also was designed to create a network to respond with love when any community faced acts of hatred—including gay bashing and immigrant persecution. The local event reminded Chris Buice of the candlelight vigil ceremony after the shooting. "Everyone was standing up and clapping," he recalled. "At that moment I had a palpable sense of love that is greater than our differences that I felt, and still feel, in a physical way."[48]

10:
Land Whoa!

Most simply, it is this: the Tennessee Valley and the continent as a whole had many riches in common when, in 1492, those riches began to be suspected. And the development of the valley up to the present has had much in common with the development of the U.S., the opening up of any rich, new land in the westward course of empire. It has been praised as a pioneer development. Other salient characteristics are these: it has been consistently short sighted, wasteful, uncoordinated. Far and wide the opinion—sound, bad, and indifferent—grows that we are approaching a turning point in civilization, that among other things an ancient human habit must be corrected. Man must learn to cooperate with his surroundings instead of disemboweling and trampling, and hoping to discard them.

—James Agee, "T.V.A.," *Fortune*, Oct. 1933, pp. 81-97.[49]

For Knox County residents who live elsewhere I explain that the 2nd District I served largely was the zone "between interstates," north of Interstate 40, east of I-275, and inside the loop of I-640, except for the Inskip neighborhood and a sliver of Fountain City that also comprise parts of the district. A better way to think of it, however, is the neighborhoods around two major arteries, Broadway and Central. The district extends all the way from where those two streets intersect near downtown to the long suburban blocks near Cedar Lane.

First Creek tumbles along its banks, crossing under Broadway several times as it winds toward the Tennessee River. Its meander bends and flood plain cut deep into the Fairmont-Emoriland neighborhood, raising concerns for the gardeners and conscientious homeowners along those manicured boulevards. Farther south the creek is forced through a concrete culvert in front of an inner-city supermarket, known locally as the Fellini Kroger (for the colorful characters one often encounters there).

The creek and its path are a microcosm of past folly in land use decisions. In a couple spots near it one still can see a remnant of the trolley tracks. These were the trolley suburbs, thriving middle and working class communities. The trolleys were abandoned, however, out of too much short-sighted affection for the automobile. Much of the middle class has moved out to more distant subdivisions. Sediment from their runoff makes this, and virtually every other creek in the county, out of statewide compliance for environmental quality. The longer commutes add tailpipe junk to the air, mixing with the effluent of upwind coal-fired power plants and leaving the air near or over the borderline of pollution standards. Oil and chemicals run off parking lots, including the abandoned "gray fields" of former big-box stores, and into the creek.

Residents do what they can about the pollution. Old North Knox Neighborhood Association puts together work Saturdays to clean litter from the creek. At one of those I found myself in bright yellow waders, working with similarly clad City Council candidate Ray Abbas, as we yanked bottles, cans, wire, metal signs, clothing, and even an old pay phone from the creek.

Neighborhood associations in the district, in fact, are an important bulwark against urban problems. Alice Bell Spring Hill Neighborhood Association is a politically savvy group, willing to work with cooperative developers but ready to fight those who do not know issues or procedures and rely on assurances and generalities. Oakwood Lincoln Park Neighborhood Association meets in a historic cabin and has worked diligently to save a historic and abandoned school building. A neighborhood group on Highland Avenue put their time, talent, and treasure to changing a vacant lot into a park.

Crashing the Commission 93

Fourth and Gill always puts on a great welcome for Knoxville Marathon participants as they run the streets of their neighborhood. That neighborhood and Old North Knox sometimes face difficulties with prostitutes, thieves, and scam artists. However, they stand up and watch out for each other. When faced with problems associated with concentration of homeless services, they adroitly balance their compassion and concern—lobbying for programs with proven track records in a scattered site model.

Fourth and Gill residents prepare to greet Knoxville Marathon runners.

Photo by Carla D. Wyrick.

Fairmont-Emoriland neighbors pushed city planners when the flooding control program faltered and sputtered. Edgewood Park's neighborhood association routinely hosts informative self-help programs. North Hills Garden club does a fantastic job of boulevard beautification. These groups were important contacts for my work as a commissioner. I'd attend their meetings and speak briefly about commission, but mostly I learned their issues, and I learned from their strength.

Individual constituents also played a big role in highlighting affronts to our community through careless land use. I met Mr. Shipley one day when I was campaigning on Freemason Street. He called me a couple years after the election to alert me to a problem. Mr. Shipley's home offered a fine view of some railroad tracks below, and a large number of tires that had been dumped there between Colonial Avenue and Hiawassee Avenue. Repeated calls to our Solid Waste officials finally yielded an answer. A tire recycler with whom the county had business had put the tires there, but the tires would be gone in two weeks. That was the assurance.

Two months passed and the tires were still there—a public health threat (mosquitoes in pooling water), an eyesore, and a fire hazard. I tried calling several local reporters, print and broadcast, as well as a few newscast producers; I'd been a TV news producer in Lubbock. It should have been a compelling tale of neighborhood threat and broken promises. I couldn't give the story away. Another week or two passed. The tires caught fire. Finally, belatedly, there was a modest amount of media interest. So a question to my friends in news: must we always wait until it's on fire? Sometimes stories are literally on fire (good pictures, I grant you), or figuratively on fire like Black Wednesday, but do we have to fall into the trap of validating the Zaller burglar alarm model? Don't we have an ethical obligation to know stories well enough and catch them early enough also to cover the fire hazards?

This time period also saw a series of underground blazes, under an illegal landfill and threatening homes on Tedford Road.[50] Another tire fire erupted at a grinding and processing facility on Boruff Street, just south of the 2nd District.[51] Solid Waste in its many forms is a major function of local governance—yes, that sh** is our business. Knox County on several occasions appeared to botch the matter. All of which brings me to Brad Mayes. He is one of those super citizens who became energized and angered by a particular action or failure of county government. He was a regular during the public forum section of commission meetings. He told us about how the county was not receiving from a solid waste/green waste/mulch contractor, Natural Resources Recovery of Tennessee, large sums of money that by most reasonable readings of the contract appeared to be an obligation. Brad, a local businessman and retail competitor to NRRT, could get distracted by side issues or take the long road to a point, but he had done a valuable public service in revealing this problem, and he had to persevere into a serious headwind of political and legal blowback. Things got so convoluted that Knox County in one lawsuit was on the side against the county getting paid what the solid waste contract indicated.

Yes, sh** happens, but why do we in government and reporting never add it up? Why, especially in news reporting, is the coverage just episodic, historical context notable for its absence? December 22, 2008, a retaining wall at the Tennessee Valley Authority's Kingston Fossil (Coal) Plant gave way. Half a billion gallons of coal ash muck, including substances like arsenic and mercury, oozed across the land and into nearby waterways. TVA estimated clean-up costs at $1.2 billion.[52] TVA then tripled the yearly salary of its president, Tom Kilgore, to $3.6 million.[53]

So why is it, after all these local developments and international crises like the months-long oil spill in the Gulf of Mexico, that environmentalism is ignored and even mocked in our local governance? Agee's 1933 quote that begins this chapter still looms large. TVA, a government project that emphasized hydroelectric power and erosion control, has moved—with a lot of local support—to a public/private, coal-dominated provider that looks and acts like the worst of our transnational energy corporations. Our neighborhood associations know environmental threats when we see them locally, and we seek government as one tool in fighting it. Political majorities in East Tennessee currently appear unwilling to extend that philosophy more broadly to our nation and our globe, but that may change slowly with each oil or ash spill, polluted stream, dirty air alert, and green field plowed under for yet another sprawl development.

Another frustration is that once a victory is won against our usual sprawl pattern, one has to keep vigilant to be certain the victory is preserved. I responded to some desperate persons in a couple rural areas, fighting against landscape businesses that had grown large next to them. Zoning did not seem to allow landscape businesses in agricultural zoning, and I got my colleagues to agree, 18-0, that was our intent. For a variety of reasons the item kept coming back to the Metropolitan Planning Commission. Twice I sat at meetings during which a chronology of the matter was presented, and the strong commission vote was left out both times. Each time I had to go to the microphone to stand up for that position and those neighbors.

Just to prove how far we have to go, new Knox County Mayor Tim Burchett fired a torpedo at the months of effort by Commissioner Tony Norman and former Knoxville City Councilman Joe Hultquist to create rules about ridge and hillside development. The pair led a task force (itself comprised of experienced persons from many points of view) that had worked with interested parties, as well as the Metropolitan Planning Commission, and held numerous public hearings. Shortly before the item was to come before the city council and county commission Burchett came out against it.[54] Commission rejected the plan on a 5-4 vote during its April 2011 meeting. A few weeks before that vote a backyard storage shed at Tony Norman's home was destroyed by fire; Tony in May spoke about the blaze, and asked the FBI to investigate what he believed to be indications of arson.[55]

11:
BZA—Cooler than it Sounds

Board of Zoning Appeals. No, it doesn't sound like a thrill a minute, and usually it isn't. At times, however, BZA could flash with anger, conflict, controversy, strangeness, intrigue, and even humor. The *Knoxville News Sentinel* rarely covered BZA. If covered at all, it would be by the *Shopper News*—a publication that sounds like a lightweight, but actually had the most insightful coverage of local government offered in the county.

BZA is where property owners interact with local government when some aspect of their property or property plans does not comply with rules. Maybe a shed is closer to the street than the main building. Perhaps a sign is too big, or parking spaces need to be a little bit smaller than standard. It is a quasi-judicial function to waive those rules. So participants are sworn, and a couple local lawyers make a decent chunk of change representing clients in the bigger and more controversial waivers sought.

BZA also could look like the ghost of commissions past. Thanks to an opinion about state law from Law Director John Owings, former commissioners removed by term limits (or, for that matter, anything else) nevertheless could remain on BZA. Thus, you could still see former commissioners Mark Cawood and Diane Jordan there and casting votes. Cawood eventually left as both member and BZA chair. The gavel went to Paul Pinkston, a sitting commissioner. Completing the political odd couple, I rose to become vice chair. That would set up some drama later, but first one of the stranger moments.

More than a Dozen Inoperable Cars

A small, frail, elderly, bespectacled woman approaches the public lectern at Knox County Board of Zoning Appeals. She's doing something unusual, appealing a fine for having too many inoperable cars on her property. The nine board members there put questions to the Law Director and the Director of Engineering. "Can we do this? What's the law on this?"

We're more accustomed to granting, rather routinely, variances to distance rules so developers can move homes away from slopes, or put swimming pools in back yards. The majority very rarely votes no, but often seeks compromise if a neighbor objects. I sometimes cast a no vote against variances for signs that are illuminated, too big, or too close to the road.

We're reminded that our zoning allows one inoperable vehicle in an agricultural lot. We barely can see the small woman behind the lectern, but she steps up on the dais to distribute pictures from around her home. She thinks she's presenting the case that there's no problem, but she's doing just the opposite. We see more than a dozen rusting cars and buses in tall grass, indicating they've been sitting there quite a while.

Her argument is a ramble of irrelevancies. The complaint is just revenge from a neighbor upset about a dog. Other nearby yards have inoperable cars, the "everybody does it" defense. Finally, she says, "He's a good boy. He just takes on a lot of projects." Her long-silent husband has been standing at her side. He finally speaks up to echo that sentiment.

At long last we are getting to the heart of the matter. It's a variation of the grown son still living in the parental home. This time it's not the lingering adolescence of the Sci-Fi fan or video gamer in the basement. Instead, he's a collector of discarded vehicles. He says not a word as the elderly parents plead on his behalf.

We try to be as sympathetic as we can, suggesting how charities will haul away junk cars and give you a tax credit.

An employee from Neighborhood Services adds the county will haul away the vehicles for free. Eventually the elderly parents agree to work with county officials to remove the car and bus carcasses.

The elderly parents shuffle out of the room, a man sporting a graying ponytail stands and walks out with them. "That must be him," Commissioner William Daniels whispers to me. "Yeah, just amazing," I mutter.

A Political Odd Couple

It's hard to explain how Paul Pinkston and I developed a surprisingly good relationship during our overlapping time on commission. Paul and his brother Howard ran a used-car operation that also was something of a political hang out. When Howard died, Paul was selected and then elected to replace him.

In the Large Assembly Room a visitor would see what approximated a large U-shaped desk serving all 19 commissioners, the open end toward the audience. My seat was audience left and Paul's was on the far right. The seating was by district number, not ideology, but one could be forgiven for thinking it was a liberal-conservative split, and that we were at or near opposing poles.

Paul is a Republican. I am a Democrat. His strongest support in his South Knoxville district is from the precincts outside the city limits. My North Knoxville district lies entirely within city limits. He never missed an opportunity to give Mayor Mike Ragsdale a hard time—at one point even taping one of their conversations. I tried to give the mayor the benefit of the doubt on several occasions, or at least not assume the worst.

My first real conversation with Paul was not encouraging. He was grumbling about the *News Sentinel*, specifically how it had maltreated him and misrepresented an issue. He wanted to yank the required public notices of meetings the county pays to place in the paper. I tried to tell him that content-based retribution against a newspaper by a government entity raised some serious First Amendment questions, but he could not be dissuaded.

During some repetitive or slow periods of long meetings I sometimes would check e-mail, blogs, or a website or two, on rare occasions even making a blog entry. During one such meeting I was explaining how I had my doubts about one of Paul's resolutions because it stepped on the legal power relationships among local, state, and federal governments. The folks at the Knoxviews website had a lot of fun with the twit trying to explain federalism to Pinkston. The site operator, Randy Neal, wrote:

> The University Twit is giving a lecture on Federalism, state and local government, and separation and balance of powers, etc., regarding a resolution to ask the State and encourage other county commissions to ask the State allow local governments to opt out of enforcing unfunded mandates, which Mark Harmon opposes.
> Pinkston says with state revenue shortfalls the state will force the county to do things the state should be doing and not funding it. He apparently didn't hear a thing Mark Harmon just said about the law.
> Passes on voice vote with one "no."
> Also just voted to request state legislature to abide by the same laws they impose on county commission (i.e. sunshine laws?). Passed unanimously.

I replied, "The New Not-Ready-For-Prime-Time Players. We started at 2:00 pm. It is now 7:44 pm. We are on the Knox County One Question Charter Amendments. These are the last items on a long agenda, though there is one person on the public comments section (if he is still here), the topic "Forced Algebra in School." Forced Civics anyone?[56]

So it was quite surprising to Paul when I nominated him

to remain as Finance Committee Chair (he already was BZA chair). My reasoning was simple. He ran a quick meeting. Nearly all of what we argued on Finance Committee would be rehashed the following Monday during the full commission meeting. Why not move quickly and just get answers to any questions we had about what was before us? He seemed to take the same approach.

Several times after that Paul would say to me, "I don't always agree with you, but I like your independence." We found common cause on a few items, especially the repeatedly disappointing performance of a contractor for solid waste, and another operator contracted to run Medicare/Medicaid certified nursing homes for the county.

Political caricatures are shorthand. It's easy to depict Paul as the caustic curmudgeon, or to present me as the nerdy professor, but who says such people, even in these stereotypes, can't work together? Sometimes authenticity trumps ideology. I have seen supposed political opposites gang up on the mushy middle. It begs the question of whether we measure too many things on simplistic scales like left to right.

So it came to pass that one day Paul wasn't feeling well. He turned the BZA gavel over to me to chair the meeting. BZA meetings never would be the same.

Bang the Gavel Firmly

The unusual non-controversial items came and went, but two big items were on the agenda and brought a larger than normal crowd to the room. The first involved a child care center in a residential area not zoned for that type of business. It was calling itself a school, trying to avoid the matter and to fend off neighborhood opposition.

A focused observer could have figured out the likely vote by the types of questions being asked. Commissioners planning to support the business, the usual pattern on commission votes, were lobbing softballs. The questions sought to find any excuse—sets of books, a stated curriculum—to call the child care business a school. I asked Joe Jarret, representing the County Law Department, whether commission could employ a balancing standard—whether the property in question was more like a child care business or more like a school. He responded that was a very reasonable standard to use. So the neighbors and I asked questions about teacher certification and other issues showing the verbal reclassification was a charade. No matter, the neighbors and I lost the vote by a wide margin.

The next big item was last on the agenda, a planned development with features very upsetting to a large number of neighbors. The area in question recently had been annexed by Knoxville, and the city agreed with the neighbors' objections. So the developer was trying to go to us, under the tenuous claim that at the start of the process the area was not within city limits.

To me it smacked of forum shopping. Why not just modify plans to mollify neighbors? So I turned to Jarret and asked, "Is it within the power of the chair to rule an item is improperly before us?"

"Yes," he said. One almost could see the blood rushing to Scoobie's head.

"I so rule," I said.

Scoobie vehemently objected and challenged the ruling of the chair. Diane Jordan already had left. Moore's potential tie-breaker was gone. The vote tied, 4-4. "The vote is four to four," I stated. "The motion fails. That being the last item before us, the committee is adjourned." I banged down the gavel. Some grateful neighbors applauded. Shortly thereafter Betty Bean, political columnist for the *Shopper News* wrote:

> I really feel compelled to commend Commissioner Mark Harmon for the yeoman's work he did as acting chair of the BZA Thursday. The odds were stacked

heavily against him, but he stood his ground, and this time he won. It's really a shame that the "big" media ignore this board, because it makes decisions that affect neighborhoods, livelihoods and quality of life issues. Mark is generally outnumbered and frequently shouted down, but he walks the walk, and as a citizen of the 2nd District, he makes me damn proud.[57]

Scoobie Don't

The final act in our BZA tragic-comedy-drama takes a twist only Knox County could imagine. County Law Director Bill Lockett had determined to his satisfaction that our operation of the BZA was in conflict with state laws. Sitting commissioners should not be serving. So we treated all past acts as de facto valid, but held hearings to place citizen BZA replacements.

The irony is that by then Scoobie had been removed from commission. A successful citizen ouster lawsuit proved to the satisfaction of a judge and later to an appeals court that he had given false statements under oath during the Sunshine Trial. So he stayed on BZA despite, in fact because, he had been removed from county commission.

My colleague Amy Broyles drafted for the full commission a resolution about future actions should commissioners be ousted. It made clear that such an ouster also would apply to boards to which the ousted person had been appointed by Knox County. She made it clear that it was not retroactive to Scoobie or anyone else, but the commission majority simply ignored that fact, continued to claim it was aimed at one person, and refused to pass the change.

Very well, I thought, then I'll draft an item that is how the majority mischaracterized Amy's resolution. I drafted a resolution to remove Scoobie from BZA. Joe Jarret wrote and briefed us all on state law and how that would proceed:

> *"For Cause"*
>
> *With respect for removal of an official or appointee from office, "for cause" constitutes some action or cause on the part of the party sought to be removed that calls into question or adversely affects the ability and fitness of the appointee to perform the duty imposed upon him, brings discredit upon the appointive authority, or engages in wrongdoing, or failure to adhere to established laws, rules, policies or procedures.*
>
> *Malfeasance is a legal term that refers to an individual intentionally performing an act that is illegal or wrong or constitutes improper conduct while in public office.*
>
> *Misfeasance is a legal act performed wrongfully. That is, a public official may do something that is not illegal but is unethical, mistaken, improper or inappropriate.*

I put both Jarret's statement and the conclusion of the ouster suit ruling on the Knox County Commissioner forum so my colleagues could see them. That ruling read:

> This Court finds by clear and convincing evidence that it strains credulity, given the heightened awareness of this appointment process by all of the Commissioners, press, and public, that Commissioner Moore would not recollect the subject matter of his phone call to Mr. Valiant. It is inconceivable to this Court that at the height of this meeting, Mr. Moore would be calling Mr. Valiant to discuss real estate. The only logical construction of these events is that as a result of Mr. Moore's call, Mr. Valiant came to the Courthouse and assisted Mr. Bolus in taking the oath of office. Mr. Valiant's actions were a result of Chairman Moore's phone calls to him. Chairman Moore's statements that he does not recall the subject matter, that it might have

been about real estate and his other explanations while under oath, were untrue. These statements were false, given under oath, intentionally, knowingly and with intent to deceive. T.C.A. 36-16-702 defines perjury as a false statement under oath. This offense is a misdemeanor, involves moral turpitude and a violation of penal statute.

Consequently, this Court orders that Commissioner Moore is hereby removed from office.[58]

Scoobie also lost an appeal of the ouster. At the meeting I also quoted from the appeal ruling.[59] Scoobie's retort could be described as a scorched earth approach. He said he had appealed his ouster to the Tennessee Supreme Court. He'd need several hours, something like eight, for his defense to BZA removal. Despite legal warnings from Law Director Joe Jarret of the futility of a defense that consists of assailing others' actions rather than addressing the matter, Scoobie tossed out a kitchen sink's worth of suspicions, assertions, and innuendo. Conflict avoidance took hold, and a majority of my colleagues voted to postpone the matter indefinitely. Rarely had I been more upset at such a vote.

The "left" side of the room. Left to right, Commissioners Sam McKenzie, Mark Harmon, Amy Broyles, Tony Norman, Ivan Harmon, and Finbarr Saunders. Why is Ivan there?

Photo by Jon Gustin.

12:
Baby you can drive my county take home vehicle

Cars to me are about utility not identity. Many of the elderly relatives in my family didn't even drive. They used Pittsburgh's trolleys or buses, or the grudging ride from my father in our family car. Those cars, Arnold and later The Shark, were named by my siblings. We had one car. My dad needed it the day I passed my driver's test. So after that proud teenage moment, I took the bus home. So it was a bit ironic but also a tad appropriate that my biggest county commission policy battle was fought over the vehicle policy.

It all started in what likely was a lingering remnant of the Hutchison-Ragsdale clashes. Scoobie had railed against the mayor having both a county-provided car and a vehicle allowance. He wanted one cut from the budget. The point had some merit but lacked the bigger scope of where else could we cut unneeded vehicles, especially take-home vehicles. I struggled with the question and voted "pass" on the measure, stating my concerns about the broader scope. The whole matter eventually led to a committee to look into the policy. The committee would be Commissioners Mike Hammond, Lumpy, and me.

Information plays a vital and underappreciated role in the success or failure of measures before county commission. Information, no matter how persuasive, cannot work miracles when it runs into strongly held or predetermined views. It can, however, carry the day on the many matters where a commissioner may hold a loose inclination or no opinion whatsoever. I kept pushing for this committee to collect a lot of information to justify a sweeping review of our policy.

Our committee held hearings, getting a good list of take-home vehicles and to whom they were assigned regarding most county offices. The sheriff's department gave a list of vehicles, but it was not as easy to piece together who had what. I visited the facility on Baxter Avenue where many county vehicles were fueled, maintained, and repaired. Commissioners Hammond looked into whether GPS systems might be a good investment. Commissioner Lambert explored vehicles assigned to judges.

This effort would turn on building a compelling case for a new policy. Online resources were quite valuable. One could find the policies of other local governments. The County Technical Assistance Service (CTAS) and Municipal Technical Assistance Service (MTAS), part of the University of Tennessee's Institute for Public Service, were valuable on this point and many others. I even found a specialized magazine, *Government Fleet*, and contacted/surveyed several fleet managers using the online survey site Survey Monkey.

The advantage goes to the prepared. A typical monthly Knox County Commission packet containing all items and all supporting documents on our agenda can exceed 2000 pages (now .pdf files, but in my first months on commission a thick printed volume delivered to one's door by a sheriff's deputy). Preparedness varied greatly by person, but it is safe to assume some areas were skimmed, if read at all. Once the sheriff's department used an interdepartmental transfer to send a county car to Law Director Bill Lockett. I'm still kicking myself on missing that one.

So often on county commission one was presented with a bad choice and a modestly better choice. Rarely was the best option even on the table. I had to find a way to get a very good option on the table, even if compromises for passage would leave a "good-not-great" policy. I saw this process at work during the debate over a Storm Water Ordinance, and even played a small role in getting some improvements into the final version. I'd also watched a series of "super citizens" come and go, people who became active when some aspect of local government disturbed their lives or offended their sensibilities. I learned from their diligent research and their persistence in the face of resistance.

Another tool available to me, and to all Knox County Commissioners, was the online commission forum. The Tennessee state legislature in the wake of Black Wednesday passed a special law allowing us to communicate with each other via a public site on which we could post messages to each other, and anyone can see what we wrote, https://knoxgov.net/commission/commissionforum/viewforum.php?f=2.

Sadly, the tool has not been used to its full potential. I tallied who used the forum since its debut on July 16, 2008, until February 1, 2011. My colleague Amy Broyles made the most combined posts and replies to posts at 69 of them. Commissioner Victoria DeFreese, who served only from the second wave of appointments until the 2008 elections, nevertheless posted 54 times. My tally was 51. Commissioner/Doctor/Colonel (no, I'm not kidding) Richard Briggs crafted 35 messages. Commissioners Mike Hammond and Paul Pinkston wrote 20 and 19 messages respectively. Tank Strickland and Lumpy Lambert posted ten times each. Sixteen other commissioners had fewer than ten posts.

	Vehicles	Law Enf.	Take Home	Take Home Law	Population	Employees	VehPerK	THPE
1	400	175	12	12	118,000	1000	3.39	0.012
2	346	83	81	77	103,000	565	3.36	0.14
3	550	250	300	250	95,000	650	5.79	0.46
4	128	46	50	35	10,000	260	12.8	0.19
5	60	23	15	3	35,000	170	1.71	0.09
6	388	177	103	80	166,000	950	2.34	0.11
7	850	382	142	142	184,000	2000	4.62	0.07
8	400	100	12	23	83,000	400	4.82	0.03
9	680	167	28	20	145,000	1000	4.69	0.03
10	154	57	3	1	43,768	411	3.52	0.01
11	815	255	75	72	166,000	1500	4.91	0.05
12	25,789	6332	1004	0	8,000,000	200,000	3.22	0.01
Knox	1200		494	361	423,874	4105	2.83	0.12

Survey Results for Comparison 2009

I made available both online and in hard copy the results of my research, including the online survey. For each community whose fleet manager responded I calculated a figure of government fleet vehicles per thousand (community population), and another ratio of take-home vehicles per thousand employees.

My careers as journalism professor and county commissioner intersect on the question of what is and isn't news. Sometimes I despair that news still operates in the way Walter Lippmann described in 1922—like a spotlight endlessly moving about, moving one development and then another out of darkness and into light. Spotlighting had some beneficial effects but is insufficient to read by or to make informed decisions, or to build a body of knowledge.[60] Too often news misses the bigger picture, but this issue of take-home vehicles had clear relevance for readers and viewers; and local news organizations responded with some good coverage. One reporter pulled a sample of 64 take-home vehicles and calculated that if Knox County had not given out SUVs and instead used smaller cars, like a Ford Focus sedan, it would have reduced fuel costs by $78,000 a year and annual CO^2 emissions by about 260 tons.[61]

The vehicle policy lurched forward, and at times it seemed like I was playing a schizophrenic game of "good cop, bad copy" with me in both roles. I don't recommend such a thing as a winning strategy, but it seemed to work in this case. Commissioner Hammond's GPS review proved the idea not cost effective. Lumpy's judicial questions never were fully explored, and at one time we got a little off topic and some folks joked about getting a county airplane. Focus and persistence were needed.

My early draft of the proposal included a specific list of persons who would lose take-home cars. The threat pushed together a series of unusual allies, including Lumpy and Mayor Ragsdale. I probably should have followed past practice of not commenting on strategy and stick to the merits, but at the meeting I could not resist a tweak that my proposal ironically had cured the rift between the mayor the sheriff's department. Mayor Mike Ragsdale exploded in anger. He took to the microphone, stated he had a great relationship with the sheriff, and he likely did with J. J. Jones. He claimed others errors. Then he went into a forceful and generic defense of his administration, talking about good jobs, real jobs – not like that job you have.

Me? Teaching isn't a real job? Or being a university professor? This guy leads a county with a major university as an employer? I held back. The whole matter was postponed to a later meeting. In the interim I dropped the references to specific persons, but beefed up the proposal with even more specifics adapted from close to a dozen other vehicle policies around the country. Joe Jarret from the Law Director's office was particularly helpful in this endeavor.

Establishment forces still rallied behind keeping their take-home cars. I received a letter dated July 9, 2009, with an unusual combined logo—on the left was the seal of the mayor's office, on the right that of the sheriff. The letter claimed no one "solicited our input on the vehicle issue," but as reporter Larry Van Guilder wrote:

> This reporter sat in on two meetings of the County Commission's ad hoc vehicle use committee in which both uniformed representatives of the sheriff's office and plenty of folks from the executive branch were in attendance.
>
> "We have been elected by the citizens to manage the day-to-day operations (of our offices)," wrote the dynamic duo. Left unsaid, but subtly implied, was the notion that Commissioner Harmon must have been elected by Martians or—worse yet—Democrats, and thus had no business meddling in their affairs.[62]

District Attorney General Randy Nichols was pressed into service at a commission meeting to denounce the list of people losing vehicles, even though he was railing against an item no longer in the proposal. Public opinion, thanks to good news coverage, seemed to a wind blowing at my back, and so I tread carefully forward—only "good cop" now. I steered clear of obstacles immune to public opinion. I had to exempt schools (not many take home vehicles anyhow, and protected from our meddling by a consent order) and sheriff's department. The vehicle policy passed 15-2. The two votes against were Commissioners Brad Anders and Greg Lambert; Paul Pinkston passed.[63]

Moments after new County Mayor Tim Burchett took the oath of office, September 1, 2010, he jangled the keys to the mayoral Chevy Tahoe, and gave them to Purchasing Director Hugh Holt. That and three other mayoral staffer cars would be sold. He had no interest in such perks.[64] Within three months Knox County had sold off 15 county vehicles at a savings of almost $92,000.[65]

13:
No Comment

Bill Lockett resigned as Knox County law director in April [2010] and pleaded guilty to pocketing more than $60,000 in clients' fees meant for his former firm, Kennerly, Montgomery & Finley, over a three-year span. His license to practice law was later suspended for four years—a decision he is appealing.

—*News Sentinel,*
Dec. 26, 2010 [66]

A jury Wednesday held a former Knox County official criminally responsible for the faking of invoices but acquitted her of a charge she used those bogus records to try to thwart a probe into abuses of taxpayer-funded purchasing cards.

After roughly four hours of deliberation, a jury in Knox County Criminal Court convicted Cynthia Finch of two counts of forgery but acquitted her of the more serious charge of fabricating evidence.

Finch, who headed the county's community services division, was the only official in former Mayor Mike Ragsdale's administration to face criminal charges in connection with the p-card scandal in which Ragsdale and his top aides made tens of thousands of dollars in questionable purchases.

—*News Sentinel,*
Jan. 27, 2011 [67]

Two Trustee's Office Employees—John Huan and Sam Harb—have been fired in connection with a Tennessee Bureau of Investigation probe of payroll irregularities... An employee in the Knox County Clerk's office, Phylicia Washington, was fired when County Clerk Foster Arnett Jr. said she tried to register a stolen vehicle. Diane Roach, an employee in the Engineering and Public Works Department, was fired for allegedly stealing $1000.

—*News Sentinel,*
May 26, 2010 [68]

The Tennessee Bureau of Investigation has confiscated records of the Knox County Trustee's office. Recently installed Trustee Fred Sisk said last month he had asked the TBI to investigate after discovering an employee had received as much as $182,000 beyond his salary and a fired operations director nearly tripled his salary last year. The Knoxville News Sentinel reported that on Monday agents took payroll records from the human resources department in the City-County Building and purchasing-card documentation from another office. Deputy county finance director Hugh Holt said his office was reviewing card purchases and the TBI seized those records as well as his office's working documents in the review.

—*Commercial Appeal,*
March 25, 2009 [69]

[Tyler] Harber, a controversial aide to former County Mayor Mike Ragsdale, left Knoxville after being accused of using his county computer and office to run political campaigns and stealing e-mails on Ragsdale's behalf. Harber is now a vice president of Wilson Research Strategies in Washington.

—*News Sentinel,*
Nov. 11, 2010 [70]

Knox County Mayor Mike Ragsdale's office charged almost $48,000 on county purchasing cards without adequate documentation, a top staffer may have fabricated receipts, and the county law director wants to do 'whatever...is necessary' to fix those and other problems raised in a preliminary audit released Thursday. This morning, Ragsdale and his staff meet with state and county auditors to begin explaining what happened. County Auditor Richard Walls, with assistance from the state Comptroller's Office, has spent nine months examining thousands of records. His draft report specifically questions purchases and expense reimbursements of Ragsdale; chief of staff Mike Arms; chief administrative officer Dwight Van de Vate; former finance director John Werner; former community services director Cynthia Finch; her former secretary, Requitta Bone; and Ragsdale's former chief executive assistant, Margie Loyd. Those seven posted charges and expenses of $209,130 from October 2002 through May 2007, but only 71 percent of that amount was documented, according to the audit. Some was repaid, but $40,678 lacked supporting receipts or documentation, and another $7,175 had insufficient documentation.

—*New Sentinel,*
Feb. 29, 2008 [71]

14:
The Moments When It Is Worth All the Trouble

Governing is not a concept or an embodiment of principles; it's not even a fulfillment of history or the crystallization of some pre-existing "will of the people." Governing is a real, live, human activity, singular each time it is brought about. At the same time it shares all the traits of everything else we do—it drains effort, uses up time, is prone to error, and occasionally rises above the petty and obvious.
 —Joseph F. Freeman, *Government is Good* (1992), p. 129.[72]

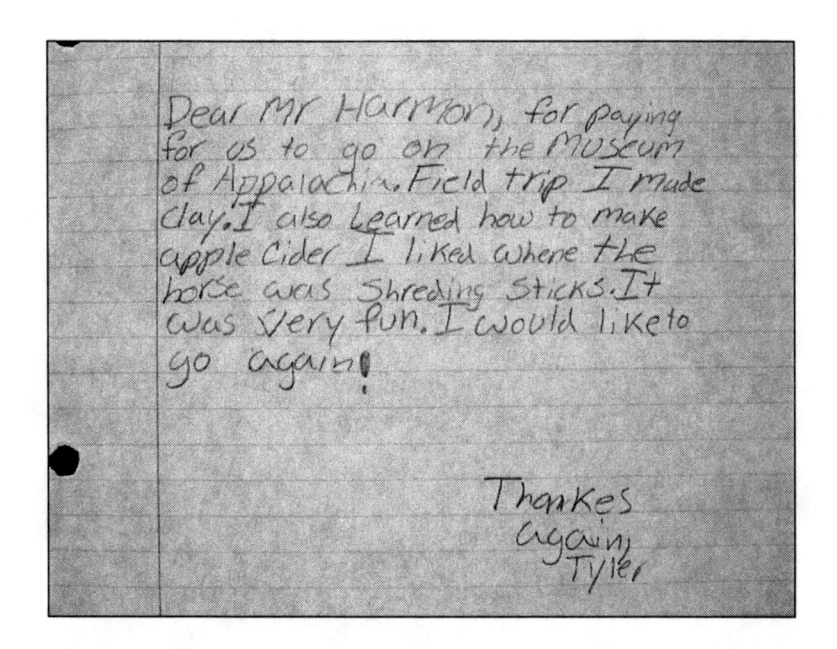

> Dear Mr Harmon, for paying for us to go on the Museum of Appalachia Field trip I made day. I also learned how to make apple cider I liked where the horse was shreding sticks. It was very fun. I would like to go again!
>
> Thankes again,
> Tyler

Knox County Commissioners have a small discretionary account, typically about $5,000 a budget year. I was pleased to use this money for various neighborhood associations, charitable groups, and special needs. One such need was underwriting the transportation for the Christenberry Elementary fourth graders to visit the Museum of Appalachia. Their teachers were kind enough to guide the kids in producing and sending to me a delightful book of photos, letters, and drawings. This was the best surprise and remains the most treasured memento of my time in office.

I failed in several budget cycles to persuade my colleagues to increase our schools spending. I pointed out other areas where cuts could be made, but could not budge a majority of commissioners—even as Knox County generally was and is below the state and national average in per pupil support. The spiral-bound fourth grader book reminds me it was worth all the effort and trouble.

Crashing the Commission 117

Dear Mr. Mark   10-9-

Thank you for giving us money to go to the Museum of Appalachia. I loved the beautiful house we got to go into. I got to go on stage and lase a rope. I learned people use to make knives out of poper trees. Thank you for giving us the money so we could go. I had a blase!

Sincerely,
September

15:
Roundin' Third and Headin' Home

I don't generally like running. I believe in training by rising gently up and down from the bench.

—Satchel Paige

Once Amy Broyles joined commission she became something of the den mother to the motley crew of men on commission. Only one other woman, Michelle Carringer, then was serving after she was appointed when Scoobie was ousted in the Seventh District. Amy planned activities for County Government Week, and prompted group activities like weight loss or fitness opportunities. She also arranged a softball tournament on Saturday, June 6, 2009, between County Commission, City Council, School Board, and the Metropolitan Planning Commission (MPC). Sheriff J.J. Jones would be the umpire. The event brought out the sports writer in me. I can't write like Red Smith, or speak like Red Barber, and can't run like Red Grange, but I did once have red hair—and my ankles were shades of red and purple after game injuries at this event. So here goes my coverage. Feel free to sing or hum John Fogerty's "Centerfield" if the spirit moves.

(Sat. June 6, 2009) The cerulean blue sky of Tyson Park gave way to an illuminated dusk before the first government softball tournament ended tonight; and the key to victory was some surprise teamwork from the county commission team.

The first tourney tilt featured Superintendent Jim McIntyre and his stubborn school board squad. Catcher Karen Carson and utility player Indya Kincannon proved tough, but the county taught them a lesson in long ball, cracking too many homers, Hugh Holt and Ivan Harmon pacing the round trippers.

"Let's play two!" cried the crowd as Knoxville City Council, in some sharp blue T-shirts, took on MPC in white. "Traitor," cried a county commission fan as Knox County's Neighborhood Services Director Grant Rosenberg batted for MPC. After the game, he was picked up on waivers by the county and all was forgiven. The rumors MPC would try to redefine the strike zone proved unfounded, but may have been their undoing. Joe Bailey's team slowly pulled away for a solid win.

The final thus was set, the inevitable clash between the city and county. Though the score ran to 12 to 10, county defense and small ball sealed the win. First basemen Larry "Stretch" Smith, relieved by Mike "The Vacuum" Brown, made secure putouts. Up the middle Tony Norman and Craig Leuthold flashed serious leather at second and center respectively. Ed Shouse in right consistently hit the cut-off man to squelch rallies.

Michelle "Road Runner" Carringer was injured by a stray city throw into the dugout, but still sped around the diamond when needed as a pinch runner. Scrappy lefty Mark Harmon punched his second single of the game over city shortstop Rob Frost, sending Tony Norman sliding home with what proved to be the game winner.

Team captain Amy Broyles batted with assistance from three-year old daughter Avery, while daughter Aidyn was batgirl. They joined the team photo as the county squad carried away the trophy.

Council members Marilyn Roddy and Bob Becker gathered their team around Joe Bailey for a photo as well. One was heard to mutter, "Say it ain't so, Joe."

Grant Rosenberg awaits the pitch.

Photo by Laura Cole.

    Knox County Commission had available throughout my time on that body some very nice collared knit short-sleeve shirts for us, each emblazoned with the county logo. The softball game was one of those few days of cooperation and collegiality when I felt great about wearing the shirt. Another such day was when Tank Strickland was going to get a kidney transplant from a generous donor match, Beverly Mulholland, a woman who went to his church.[73] In honor of both of them we arranged to have a blood donation event in the Large Assembly Room of the City County Building. Several of us joined county workers in donating a lot of blood that day.

16:
NIMBY, the Homeless, and Political Identity

In order to accomplish all—or any—of these things [superior schools, vibrant downtown, cleaner environment], Knoxvillians would have to do considerably more than talk about their common opportunities and challenges. In short, they would have to begin thinking as citizens of a city, not as their rural ancestors had thought. They would have to embrace a new system of values that, at crucial times, would put the good of the whole community above their individual self-interests. Then, armed with new ways of thinking and a new sense of civic and personal responsibility, they would have to rise up on their hind legs and shout down the cynics and naysayers. In truth, if Knoxville was the way it was because their forbears had wanted it so, then they must summon the will to make a new city.

—William Bruce Wheeler,
Knoxville, Tennessee: A Mountain City in the New South, 2nd edition,
University of Tennessee Press, 2005, p. 202.

The room is filling quickly. People are standing in the back on a small raised dais normally used to lead senior exercise classes. Knox County's Neighborhood Services Director Grant Rosenberg is sitting by the laptop and Power Point projector. The screen is white with only small lettering at the bottom with the basics, "Public Meeting, Strang Senior Center, 11 12 09." No need to say more. No need for graphics. No need to antagonize before things begin. I see some people who are advocating creating a residence for formerly homeless persons on Debusk Lane in West Knoxville, but the crowd looks like it overwhelmingly is in opposition. It could even get ugly. Suddenly in this very Republican enclave I'm very aware of the tie I am wearing. It has lots of small donkeys on it.

NIMBY (Not in My Back Yard) has a long political history. It can be a force for good, like stopping a toxic dump near a school, but it also can be a reflection of our worst fears about one another in political form, a nasty outburst not really amenable to logical debate. I was afraid this meeting was drifting inexorably toward the latter.

In politics your allies can cause you so much more angst than your opponents, and so it was that I cringed several times at the political tin ear of Jon Lawler, director of the Ten-Year Plan to End Chronic Homelessness, and David Arning of Southeastern Housing Foundation, developer of the planned 23-apartment building. Too often they'd give answers that were legally correct, but not attuned to questioner concerns. At one point Arning said, "You don't have any say in where they [formerly homeless] live, just as you don't have a say in where African-Americans live." Yes, true, but there is a question of a grant that commission can approve or deny. Furthermore, don't imply people are being discriminatory, assume the best of intent and respond that way. He could have said something like, "This isn't going to be a shelter; it's going to be a home—a home for someone selected as having the best potential to start a better life—and with supervision and services that are important to that person and to making the program work for him and you."

Ginny Weatherstone of Volunteer Ministry Center was giving answers like that, but she had too big a mountain to climb; the 200 attending became increasingly agitated and their worst suspicions were allowed to fester almost unchecked.[74]

At the commission meeting the commissioners from West Knoxville took conciliatory steps to keep the angry aspects at bay while pushing cost questions. I called those questions "bogus," and pointed out that the savings from permanent supportive housing (versus homeless on the street) for 23 people meant that the project would pay for itself in less than two years. This wasn't about money, I said, this was about geography and fear. Crickets. The meeting proceeded as if that point hadn't been made. Beth Booker, a mother and cancer survivor, spoke emphatically from the audience microphone for shared community response and a scattered site approach. Her reward was being called a "bitch" by someone in the crowd as Beth returned to her seat. The commission voted 15 to 4 to kill the proposal.[75]

My relationship with the Ten Year Plan has been a supportive but conflicted one. I had an early meeting with its leaders regarding a permanent supportive housing site that would also be a historic renovation, Minvilla. It was too close to the cluster of homeless services in one area. I believed Amy and I had an agreement that TYP leaders would support my amendment for a "two-mile radius," In other words, TYP would, as a condition of the Minvilla contract, agree not to seek grants for future sites within two miles of that location.

At the commission meeting those same leaders were not interested in the amendment, and then Law Director Bill Lockett and I started a running dispute over whether such a condition in a contract would violate the Fair Housing Act. I even went to his office with a list of legal cases supporting my point of view. While spirited, it all became a moot point. Commission eventually passed the Minvilla grant without my amendment. The TYP leaders, to their credit, did start to find locations that truly represented a scattered site approach. TYP won a battle in Knoxville City Council for a location at a former South Knox school, but the forces of reaction were building. When new mayor Tim Burchett came into office in late 2010, he further and needlessly complicated matters by insisting any county support was contingent on a no-alcohol policy at any site. Research suggests that isn't the way to go. It's far better to have a mixed policy, some with alcohol restrictions, and some in which the residents are not forced to that position, but possibly get there on their own—typically a more lasting change in behavior.

As Knoxville's Mayor Bill Haslam left town to become Tennessee's governor, he gave a farewell address that easily could be viewed as a swipe at new Knox County Mayor Tim

Burchett's mucking up the homeless plans with Burchett's insistence that no alcohol be present in any of the apartment homes. Haslam said:

> We must continue to find the best practices to effectively deal with homelessness. It is a major issue for our city and our community. I believe that permanent supportive housing is the right approach. We must not forget, however, that it is not the only tenet of the Ten Year Plan. The plan has given us better ways to work at effectively dealing with the problems of homelessness in our community. And it is working. It is essential that we continue to search out and implement methods to prevent and address the day to day challenges homelessness present, and we must not let homelessness become an issue that divides us and appeals to the worst of our impulses.[76]

At this writing serious work on homeless issues has been forced back to its previous starting point of community meetings. The Ten Year Plan is no more, replaced by Compassion Knoxville, a task force originally co-chaired by TYP supporter Stephanie Matheny and TYP opponent Ron Peabody. Peabody left the task force when he launched a bid for Knoxville City Council.[77] The 20 people on the task force valiantly press forward with efforts to get some consensus and some action.

The events regarding the Ten Year Plan to End Chronic Homelessness align with the valuable political observations of George Lakoff in his book *Don't Think of an Elephant*. He pointed out that conservatives take a "stern father" approach to understanding the world around them. The world is a dangerous place. People have bad instincts and must be taught right. People who are successful have achieved such status by moral uprightness and good choices. People who are not well off such as the poor and homeless, conversely, are in such a state because of some personal or moral failing. Liberals or progressives tend to see multiple causes and links to societal problems in poverty and homelessness, and follow more of a nurturing family model in defining potential solutions.[78]

A small part of my academic research (you know, all that university twit stuff) has included re-analyzing dozens of existing public opinion polls to see if the Lakoff observation holds true over time and in multiple environments. It does, and at highly significant levels, consistently and overwhelmingly.[79]

Understanding these political tendencies is useful, but not sufficient to devise persuasive arguments to change minds about permanent supportive housing in suburban neighborhoods. Fear is a powerful motivation, one that most elected politicians recognize and do not want to find themselves on the opposite side of it. As Upton Sinclair once noted, "It is difficult to get a man to understand something, when his salary depends upon his not understanding it!"[80]

17:
Decommissioned

To lead the people walk behind them.

—Lao Tzu

Photo by Jon Gustin.

The *Shopper News'* Larry Van Guilder suffered through enough tedious commission meetings for several lifetimes. That's why I treasure this item from his 2009 reporter's Christmas list:

> A new university twit. Mark Harmon's departure from commission will leave that body gasping for logic. Dubbed a university twit by (who else?) Lumpy, Harmon may hold the commission record for casting votes for the losing side.

But that's a good thing, because in nearly every instance, Harmon has advocated for the right cause. The academy and a legislative body aren't always the most comfortable of partners, but Harmon deserves credit for bringing his research skills to bear on such issues as the county vehicle policy.

The loyal opposition deserves a passionate voice. Amy Broyles, Sam McKenzie, Tony Norman, or Finbarr Saunders may fill the void. If they don't, please Santa, send me a professor.[81]

Public referendum changed the County Charter so the commission was reduced from 19 members to 11, from two per district to one. I mulled the matter, but chose not to seek a second term. I did not want to go head-to-head against my friend Amy Broyles. She had served but two years and was doing a good job. I would complete one full term, true to my pledge to constituents that I didn't want to make a career of this—just do some good in a term or two and move on.

This book is called *Crashing the Commission*, and the word play is intentional. Yes, I was an outsider, not born here and not raised here. I also was a party crasher to a calcified commission desperately clinging to old ways, old power bases, and long-term players. Despite what happened on Black Wednesday and in the Sunshine Trial, I did not bring the commission crashing down. It crashed of its own failings, and deserved all the derision heaped upon it. Our community rebuilt its self-governance and is better for it.

Of course, the subtitle is *Confessions of a University Twit* (thanks Lumpy). So, true to my academic roots, I need to take note of the bigger questions and answers. The American ideal of local governance can be traced to Alexis de Tocqueville and his praise for how a New England townsman is attached to his township. "He takes part in every occurrence in the place; he practices the art of government in the small sphere within his reach; he accustoms himself to those forms without which liberty can only advance by revolution; he imbibes their spirit; he acquires a taste for order, comprehends the balance of powers, and collects clear practical notions on the nature of his duties and the extent of his rights."[82]

The reality of county government, however, is quite a bit different from the ideal. Henry S. Gilbertson got so upset at the hodgepodge of county government structure that he called counties "the dark continent of American politics."[83] Robert Lorch's text about state and local government put it well:

> The typical county elects a row of major officials who manage their own departments without any chain-of-command supervision from a higher authority in the county. Seldom does any "higher authority" exist, except, of course, the voting public. Elected officials are czars of their own little semiautonomous government. The sheriff, for example, is not answerable to anyone, not even the so-called county board which is often erroneously believed to "govern" the county. Some exceptions to this chaotic picture exist. A few counties have been streamlined, but it is not easy to streamline a county or to reorganize any governmental apparatus. Each such apparatus is a nucleus of political power, and each has a robust instinct for survival.[84]

Structural flaws can set up problems, but inattention by voters and malfeasance by office holders are the key human elements in local government failures. "The decisive factors in shaping the ultimate pattern of government are not the authorizing charters but the political methods of the citizenry," Duane Lockard properly noted.[85]

Knox County paid for a generous deputy pension by borrowing, adding interest to a debt and pushing the problem down the road. Knox County also lost money to careless oversight of purchasing cards and excess generosity with take-home vehicles. The scale of those problems, however, pales in comparison to what happened in Orange County.

The Orange County bankruptcy was by far the biggest municipal bankruptcy in history at $1.64 billion. Never before had a major municipality declared bankruptcy, though a few rural governments had. Mark Baldassare investigated the 1998 crash and its generalizability:

> The Orange County bankruptcy merits scrutiny because the same problems could be repeated in other municipalities throughout the United States. Orange County is not the only municipality where local officials are searching for creative ways to increase their revenues in order to provide more public services. Many local governments are operating under tight fiscal conditions. Elected officials in numerous locales are faced with voters' demands for more public services and their unwillingness to pay higher taxes. Other local governments also have structures that allow public figures to operate with great autonomy and little fiscal oversight. It is thus important to identify the lessons to be learned from the Orange County experience.[86]

About six months before the bankruptcy, 600 Orange County voters were asked "When it comes to Orange County leaders, what names comes to mind?" 56% could name no one, 22% one leader, 11% two, only 11% could name three. When it came to favorable or unfavorable views of each of the five-member Board of Supervisors, don't knows ranged from 58 to 74%.[87]

One formal poll about Knox County Commission, seven months after its implosion, followed the pattern of other local governments. Vague uncertainty may prevail about its roles, players, and importance, but heightened annoyance rises when the "burglar alarm" is clanging. That alarm clearly was clanging in 2007. Seven in ten respondents rated the overall performance of Knox County government as fair or poor. More than three in four rated Knox County Commission as fair or poor, and nearly 56 percent said their evaluation of commission had become more negative in the past year. More than nine in ten respondents said they were "aware of the controversy about the way in which the County Commission replaced term-limited members earlier this year," and more than two-thirds said the controversy changed their opinion of how well the commission was doing its job.

In the same survey three in four respondents were aware of the lawsuit about how the commission replaced the term-limited; of those who knew, four in five favored it. Other specific remedies were more fragmented. One in four wanted to re-do appointments, nearly 17% wanted to recall the entire commission, and about 18% wanted to leave things alone until the election. The question may have left out too many other options (special election, reconfiguration of government structure) because two in every five respondents gave an answer coded as "other."

The survey asked about three people. Mayor Ragsdale and his Director of Community Services, Cynthia Finch, both scored low in approval. Only 302 of 697 respondents said they had heard of Scott Moore. Of those, only 109 precisely named him as the chair, another 44 said he was on commission. The remainder didn't know or named another title. The poll reported only five respondents gave Moore an excellent rating; 14 good, 49 fair; 76 poor. Only eight reported they held a more positive opinion of Moore over the past year, 76 said more negative, and 82 reported no change in their opinion. No other individual commissioners were mentioned in the poll.[88]

Lingering voter resolve to clean house also may be inferred from the next opportunity voters had on these matters. In the February 2008 Republican Primary Scott Moore secured less than 17% of the vote in his effort to become the next county clerk. Lee Tramel, for whom great effort was extended as he became a Black Wednesday appointee, raised $42,440 and spent extensively on radio, TV, and newspaper ads; he received 1,091 votes (17.79%), a cost of $38.86 per vote. The Law Director during Black Wednesday, John Owings, and ex-trustee Mike Lowe vastly outspent their respective opponents, but both still lost. Bi-Lo consensus candidate and Black Wednesday appointee in the district serving South Knoxville, Tim Greene, also lost.[89]

On the Democratic side of the primary the woman I called the "people's choice" proved to be precisely that. Amy Broyles faced two primary challengers and still secured more than 59% of the vote, carrying every precinct in the second district. Chuck Bolus, he of the Black Wednesday early swearing in but failing memory for how it happened, was unopposed in the Republican primary. I was astounded during that summer to see one of his bumper stickers. It read re-elect Charles Bolus. Re-elect?! The public hadn't elected him to anything. Amy Broyles beat him in the August 2008 general election, getting almost 62% of the vote and again carrying every precinct.[90] On many levels the verdict of the people matched the verdict of the Black Wednesday jurors. That didn't mean the commission majority would agree to ease the path for a citizen initiative to change the structures of county government. That would require a petition drive to get the matter before voters.

Shortly after the election drubbing, Scott Moore resigned as commission chairman, and the vice chair, Thomas "Tank" Strickland, rose to the challenge. We, his colleagues, kept the soft-spoken and patient Tank in that spot until his term ended.

Under normal circumstances only political hobbyists or players, or those dragged into conflicts, may know the participants well enough to analyze their efforts. I was pleased to spend four years experiencing this important subset of self-governance and to learn what it reveals in its ordinary and dysfunctional moments about human and organizational behavior.

Not many people get to write and to sing their own swan song, but thanks to the East Tennessee chapter of the Society of Professional Journalists I was able to do so on July 24, 2010. The event was the Front Page Follies, an annual event to raise money for journalism scholarships. The dinner and auction close with a series of musical numbers making fun of local politics and politicians. As one of those politicians, and as a journalism professor, I was welcomed as a special cast member. In the closing number, "50 Ways to Leave the Limelight," I walked from backstage, the tune changed to MacArthur Park, and I warbled:

> Mark Harmon's part
> Is melting in the dark.
> All my sweet, green platform voted down.
> Someone left debate out of the game.
> I don't think that I can take it
> 'Cause I can't sing but I fake it
> I may never get this chance to serve again. Oh no!

The applause was generous and encouraging. One month later was my last commission meeting. All the departing persons were honored and spoke briefly. I mentioned that four years ago Commissioners Greg Lambert, Phil Ballard, and I were in a car headed to Nashville to attend a statewide CTAS seminar on our new jobs. No, this was not the set up to political sketch comedy. It really happened. A lot of later speakers wished they could have eavesdropped on that conversation. All I said was that after the last four years, quoting the Grateful Dead, "lately it occurs to me what a long, strange trip it's been."

A few weeks later Becky was in our front yard as our sharp-witted letter carrier approached our mailbox. For the past four years he had been delivering commissioner mail addressed to the Honorable Mark Harmon. "Guess he's not honorable any more," the mailman joked. "That's right," chuckled Becky.

Now more than a year removed from county commission I still get some "honorable" mail. Some acquaintances and friends ask, "Are you still on city council?" Sometimes I correct and mention county commission. Mostly I just say it's nice to watch meetings with a mute button.

Notes

[1] Arthur W. Bromage, "Notes on Rural Local Government: The Crisis of County Government in Michigan," *The American Political Science Review*, Vol. 25, No.1, Feb. 1931, p. 135.

[2] Molly Ivins, "Lubbock: Seat of Rebellion," *Texas Monthly*, May 1989, p. 106.

[3] Betty Bean, "A different kind of commissioner," *Bearden Shopper-News*, Aug. 16, 2010, p. A4.

[4] Editorial Board, "Take the time to vote in today's election," *Knoxville News Sentinel*, Aug. 3, 2006, p. B4.

[5] Georgiana Vines, "Early returns don't look good for 'big orange' ballot challengers," *Knoxville News Sentinel*, Aug. 4, 2006, p. A12.

[6] Scott Barker, "All incumbents but one appear to have won—Knox County Commission," *Knoxville News Sentinel*, Aug. 4, 2006, p. A1.

[7] H. L. Mencken, *The American Language, Supplement I*, New York: Alfred A. Knopf, 1945, p. 282.

[8] Molly Ivins, "Wiggy Republicans," *Mother Jones*, Sept./Oct. 1992, p. 9.

[9] See Deanne N. Den Hartog, Jaap J. Van Muijen, and Paul L Koopman, *Journal of Occupational & Organizational Psychology*, March 1997, Vol. 70 Issue 1, pp. 19-34.

[10] Associated Press, "Tenn. Commissioners: God is foundation," Dec. 23, 2007, First Amendment Center, http://www.firstamendmentcenter.org/news.aspx?id=19480. Visited Feb. 1, 2011.

[11] Available on YouTube, http://www.youtube.com/watch?v=POCnXebRQno. Viewed Feb. 21, 2011.

[12] Editorial, "Lambert should stay out of the audience," *Knoxville News Sentinel*, April 3, 2009, p. 16; Ansley Haman and Rebecca Ferrar, "Finch accuses media, commission of racism," *Knoxville News Sentinel*, Jan. 10, 2008, p. 1.

[13] Rebecca Ferrar, "Norman warns colleague," *Knoxville*

News Sentinel, July 18, 2009, p. 1; Rebecca Ferrar, "Lambert censured," *Knoxville News Sentinel*, July 28, 2009, p. 1.

[14] Staff reports, "Chronology of events in term limits, open meetings," *Knoxville News Sentinel*, Oct. 3, 2007, pp. 8-9.

[15] Rebecca Ferrar, "Ragsdale calls ruling a 'victory,'" *Knoxville News Sentinel*, Jan. 13, 2007, p. 1; Scott Barker, "What's Next," *Knoxville News Sentinel*, Jan. 13, 2007, p. 1.

[16] News Sentinel Staff, "Commission rejects voter input to fill spots," Jan. 22, 2007, Knoxnews.com. Viewed Jan. 23, 2007; Amelia Daniels, "Knox Co. commission settles on appointment process for next week," Jan. 22, 2007, wate.com. Viewed Jan. 23, 2007; Rebecca Ferrar, "Attorney urges openness," *Knoxville News Sentinel*, Jan. 22, 2007, pp. A1, A8; Anonymous, "The Moore things change, the Moore they stay the same..." *Knoxville Voice*, Jan. 25, 2007, p. K12; Rebecca Ferrar, "No special election or nonbinding vote," *Knoxville News Sentinel*, Jan. 23, 2007, pp. A1, A5.

[17] Editorial, "Commission appointments: What public?" *Knoxville News Sentinel*, Feb. 1, 2007, p. B4.

[18] Mark Harmon, Knoxnews, "Press Release: Commissioner Mark Harmon on Monday's forum," Jan. 31, 2007. http://www.knoxnews.com/news/2007/jan/31/bpress-releaseb-commissioner-mark-harmon-on/. Viewed Jan. 31, 2007.

[19] Molly Ivins, *Molly Ivins Can't Say That, Can She?* New York: Random House, 1991, p. 69.

[20] Rebecca Ferrar, "400 onlookers watch 'circus' of recesses, private votes," *Knoxville News Sentinel*, Feb. 1, 2007. Knoxnews, viewed Feb. 4, 2011.

[21] Rebecca Ferrar, "400 onlookers watch 'circus' of recesses, private votes," *Knoxville News Sentinel*, Feb. 1, 2007. Knoxnews, viewed Feb. 4, 2011.

[22] Dan Barry, "Backroom Politics Is Brought to the People,

and the People Step In," *The New York Times*, Feb. 4, 2008, p. 12.

[23] Jamie Satterfield, "Talks, deals recounted," *Knoxville News Sentinel*, July 29, 2007, p. 15.

[24] Phil Guthe, *Term Limits, the book*, Knoxville, Tennessee: author self-published, 2010, p. 142.

[25] Mark Harmon deposition, Sunshine Lawsuit, Gibson Court Reporting, p. 25.

[26] Jamie Satterfield, "Harmon becomes star witness for sunshine plaintiffs, exposes secrecy," *Knoxville News Sentinel*, Sept. 20, 2007, knoxnews.com, viewed Feb. 1, 2011.

[27] Staff reports, "Chronology of events in term limits, open meetings," *Knoxville News Sentinel*, Oct. 3, 2007, pp. 8-9.

[28] Rebecca Ferrar, "400 onlookers watch 'circus' of recesses, private votes," *Knoxville News Sentinel*, Feb. 1, 2007. Knoxnews, viewed Feb. 4, 2011.

[29] Greg Johnson, "The good, the bad and phew," *Knoxville News Sentinel*, Feb. 2, 2007, p. 15.

[30] Dan Barry, "Backroom Politics Is Brought to the People, and the People Step In," *The New York Times*, Feb. 4, 2008, p. 12.

[31] Lisa Sandberg, "Noted Texas liberal Molly Ivins dies," *Houston Chronicle*, Jan. 31, 2007. Houston Chronicle Online, viewed Feb. 14, 2011; Katharine Q. Seelye, "Molly Ivins, Columnist, Dies at 62," *New York Times*, Feb. 1, 2007; Wade Goodwyn, "Treasuring the Wit and Wisdom of Molly Ivins," National Public Radio, Feb. 1, 2007, npr.org, viewed, Feb. 14, 2011; Kelley Shannon, Associated Press, "Syndicated columnist Molly Ivins dies at 62," msnbc.com and washingtonpost.com, both viewed Feb. 14, 2011.

[32] John Zaller, "A New Standard of News Quality: Burglar Alarms for the Monitorial Citizen," *Political Communication*, 2003, pp. 109-130.

[33] Jamie Satterfield, "Harmon accused of political agenda,"

Knoxville News Sentinel, Sept. 20, 2007, p. A11.

34 Jamie Satterfield, "Harmon accused of political agenda," *Knoxville News Sentinel*, Sept. 20, 2007, pp. A1, A11.

35 Jamie Satterfield, "Harmon accused of political agenda," *Knoxville News Sentinel*, Sept. 20, 2007, pp. A1, A11.

36 Rebecca Ferrar, "Government's a family affair," *Knoxville News Sentinel*, Feb. 18, 2007 (online chart updated Aug. 22, 2007), Knoxnews.com, http://www.knoxnews.com/news/2007/feb/18/governments-a-family-affair/ Viewed Feb. 26, 2011.

37 Jack McElroy, "Winds of change have blown through Knox County," [editorial] *Knoxville News Sentinel*, Sept. 5, 2010, p. 60.

38 Georgiana Vines, "Tension unwinds between commissioners," *Knoxville News Sentinel*, Feb. 25, 2008, p. 9.

39 Jim Gray, "Group paid a price for democracy in Knox County," *Knoxville News Sentinel*, June 21, 2009, p. 59.

40 Also see Herbert Sydney Duncombe, *County Government in America*, Washington, D.C.: NACo Research Foundation, 1966, p. 20; William A. Giles, Gerald T. Gabris, and Dale A. Crane, " The Uniqueness of County Government" *Public Administration Review*, Vol. 40, No. 1 (Jan.-Feb., 1980), p. 24.

41 Betty Bean, "Should the Media be Grammar Nannies?" July 17, 2007, Knoxviews, http://www.knoxviews.com/node/5099. Viewed, January 21, 2011.

42 Dan Barry, "Backroom Politics Is Brought to the People, and the People Step In," *The New York Times*, Feb. 4, 2008, p. 12.

43 Steve Drevik, "Reforming County Commission in the Fourth District," http://reform4.blogspot.com/, entry for Monday, July 28, 2008, viewed January 11, 2011.

44 Travis Loller, Associated Press, "Knoxville church spurs 'love' project," *Knoxville News Sentinel*, Feb. 13, 2011.

45 Mark D. Harmon, "Bias? Arrogance? Goldberg Liberal Media Claims Fail Logical Tests," *The Review of Com-*

munication, a refereed online journal, April-August 2005, pp. 109-118.

[46] *Washington Post,* "The attack and aftermath," http://www.washingtonpost.com/wp-srv/special/politics/giffords-shooting-timeline/ Viewed Feb. 12, 2011; *CBS News,* "Victims of the Tucson Shooting Rampage," http://www.cbsnews.com/ stories/2011/01/08/national/main7226900.shtml. Viewed Feb. 12, 2011.

[47] Natalie Neysa Alund, "Kiffin bobblehead dolls granted pardon—Doll shooting event now a charity adoption," *Knoxville News Sentinel*, Jan. 15, 2011, p. A1; WBIR TV, "Another charity declines to accept proceeds of 'Shoot at Lane Kiffin Bobblehead' event," Jan. 14, 2011, wbir.com, viewed Jan. 14, 2011.

[48] Travis Loller, Associated Press, "Knoxville church spurs 'love' project," *Knoxville News Sentinel*, Feb. 13, 2011.

[49] Quoted in Paul Ashdown's *James Agee: Selected Journalism*, Knoxville, TN: University of Tennessee Press, 2005, p. 13.

[50] Jim Balloch, "Fires at dump turn into never-ending headache," *Knoxville News Sentinel*, May 18, 2008, p. 17; Jim Balloch, "Illegal landfill fire costly; plan to fill, cap site will save county millions on cleanup," *Knoxville News Sentinel*, Sept. 6, 2009, p. 17.

[51] Bob Fowler, "Site of tire fire under investigation," *Knoxville News Sentinel*, May 2, 2009, p. 1.

[52] Shaila Dewan, "T.V.A. to Pay $43 Million On Projects In Spill Area," *The New York Times*, Sept. 15, 2009, p. 13.

[53] Randall Higgins, "TVA responds to county's resolution about agency's 'excessive salaries,'" *Chattanooga Times Free Press*, Dec. 30, 2010, p. A5.

[54] Staff, "Burchett opposes Knox hillside plan," *Knoxville News Sentinel*, Feb. 26, 2011, p. A4.

[55] Hayes Hickman, "Knox Commissioner Norman says blaze at his home was intimidation," *Knoxville News Sentinel*, May 11, 2011, p. 1.

[56] Mark Harmon, Randy Neal, and other thread participants. "Knox County Commission Underway," April 28, 2008, Knoxviews, http://www.knoxviews.com/node/7749. Viewed January 11, 2011.

[57] Betty Bean, "Mark Harmon is My Commissioner," Dec. 18, 2008, Knoxviews http://www.knoxviews.com/node/9953. Viewed Jan. 14, 2011.

[58] Ruling by Judge Jon Kerry Blackwood, Chancery Court of Knox County, Tennessee, No. 171426-2, Entered Oct. 14, 2008.

[59] State of Tennessee ex rel. Robert L. Wolfenbarger, III, et al., v. Scott Moore, et al. Appeal from the Chancery Court of Knox County. Hershel Pickens Franks, P.J., delivered the opinion of the Court, in which D. Michael Swiney, J., and John W. McClarty, J., joined. No. E2008-02545-COA-R3-CV. Filed Feb. 12, 2010.

[60] Walter Lippmann, *Public Opinion*, New York: Simon & Schuster, reproduced as Chapter 3 "Newspapers" in *Media Power in Politics, 4th edition*, Doris A. Graber, editor. Washington, DC: CQ Press, 2000.

[61] Larry Van Guilder, "Take me home, county car," *Shopper-News*, Aug. 4, 2008, p. A1.

[62] Larry Van Guilder, "Greetings from the shayor and the meriff," *Shopper-News*, July 20, 2009, p. A4.

[63] Mark Harmon, "Non-Lumpy Commission Notes," Knoxviews, July 27, 2009, http://www.knoxviews.com/node/11809. Viewed Feb. 22, 2011.

[64] Mike Donilla (and photo by Michael Patrick), "Knox County Mayor Burchett vows to rein in costs," *Knoxville News Sentinel*, Sept. 2, 2010, p. 1.

[65] Mike Donilla, "Mayor's office sells 15 county vehicles," *Knoxville News Sentinel*, Dec. 5, 2010, p. B8

[66] Staff, "Top Stories of 2010," *Knoxville News Sentinel*, Dec. 26, 2010, p. B1.

[67] Jamie Satterfield, "Finch verdict split—Ex-official guilty of forgery, acquitted of obstructing probe," *Knoxville News*

Sentinel, Jan. 27, 2011, p. A1.

[68] Editorial, "Corruption is a cancer on public service," *Knoxville News Sentinel*, May 26, 2010, p. 16.

[69] Associated Press, "Around the Region," *The* (Memphis) *Commercial Appeal*, March 25, 2009, p. B5.

[70] Staff, "Local Boy Makes Bad," *Knoxville News Sentinel*, Nov. 11, 2010, p. AA13.

[71] Ansley Haman, "Audit questions $48,000 in charges," *Knoxville News Sentinel*, Feb. 29, 2008, p. 1.

[72] Joseph F. Freeman, *Government is Good*, Columbia, Missouri: University of Missouri Press, 1992, p. 129.

[73] Kristi L. Nelson, "On the road to recovery," *Knoxville News Sentinel*, March 28, 2009, p. 4.

[74] Rebecca Ferrar, "200 voice their opposition to apartments for homeless," *Knoxville News Sentinel*, Nov. 13, 2009, p. 1.

[75] J. J. Stambaugh, "West Knox site out," *Knoxville News Sentinel*, Nov. 17, 2009, p. 1.

[76] Betty Bean, "Haslam bids Knoxville adieu," *Shopper-News*, Jan. 10, 2011, p. 4.

[77] Rebecca Ferrar, "Compassion Knoxville: Let's talk—Group fighting homelessness plans meetings," *Knoxville News Sentinel*, April 8, 2011, p. 18; Pam Strickland, op-ed column, "Compassion Knoxville gathers input on homeless," *Knoxville News Sentinel*, May 20, 2011, p. B3; Rebecca Ferrar, "Homeless plan critic to run for Knoxville City Council seat," *Knoxville News Sentinel*, June 10, 2011, p. 6.

[78] Lakoff, George. *Don't Think of an Elephant: Know Your Values and Frame the Debate*. White River Junction, VT: Chelsea Green Publishing, 2004.

[79] Mark Harmon, "When Mediated Poverty Stereotypes align with Public Opinion: a Clear Predictor of Ideology and Party in the U.S." Paper presented to the annual meeting of the Midwest Political Science Association, Chicago, Illinois, 2010; Mark Harmon, "Why People are Poor/

Wealthy: Powerful Frames." Poster presented to the 7th International Conference on Conceptions of Library and Information Science, London, UK, June 23, 2010.
[80] Upton Sinclair, *I, Candidate for Governor: And How I Got Licked* (1935), reprinted by University of California Press, 1994, p. 109.
[81] Larry Van Guilder, "A Reporter's Christmas List," *Shopper-News*, Nov. 30, 2009, p. A4.
[82] Alexis deTocqueville, *Democracy in America*, translated by Henry Reeve, edited with notes by Francis Bowen. Boston, Massachusetts: John Allyn Publisher, 6th ed., 1876, pp. 85-86.
[83] Henry S. Gilbertson. *The County, the "Dark Continent" of American Politics*, New York: The National Short Ballot Association, 1917.
[84] Robert S. Lorch. *State and Local Politics, The Great Entanglement*, Englewood Cliffs, New Jersey: Prentice-Hall, Inc., 1983, p. 253.
[85] Duane Lockard. *The Politics of State and Local Government, 2nd edition*, New York: The Macmillan Company, p. 6.
[86] Mark Baldassare. *When Government Fails, The Orange County Bankruptcy*, Berkeley, California: University of California Press and Public Policy Institute of California, 1998, p. 5.
[87] Mark Baldassare. *When Government Fails, The Orange County Bankruptcy*, Berkeley, California: University of California Press and Public Policy Institute of California, 1998, p. 55.
[88] Michael Gant, Social Science Research Institute, University of Tennessee, Knoxville, conducted Aug. 28 to Sept. 2, as well as Sept. 4 and 5, 2007, 697 Knox County residents interviewed, margin of error +/ 3.71% at the 95% confidence level. Available at http://www.knoxnews.com/news/2007/sep/07/70-say-county-needs-to-improve/ and http://www.knoxnews.com/news/2007/sep/06/poll-dissat-

isfaction-high-knox-county-government-l/, as file named 0906knox-county-poll.pdf. Viewed Feb. 23, 2011.

[89] Jack McElroy, editorial, "Few survivors left on our island," *Knoxville News Sentinel*, Feb. 10, 2008, p. 70; Greg Johnson, editorial columnist, "Republicans rage against the machine," *Knoxville News Sentinel*, Feb. 8, 2008, p. 17; Knox County election results available through the Knox County Election Commission.

[90] Knox County election results available through the Knox County Election Commission.

MARK D. HARMON served from 2006 to 2010 as a Knox County Commissioner, representing the second district during a time of great turmoil: a crisis stemming from ignored term limits, a successful sunshine lawsuit about botched appointments to office, and a politically motivated shooting at his church.

Harmon is a professor of journalism and electronic media at the University of Tennessee, Knoxville. He is the author of a book about news coverage of antiwar veterans, several book chapters, and dozens of articles, both popular and academic, in national and international publications.